Christmas is the Season of the Year When ...

A Thought for Each Day of the Year

Philip M. Hudson

Copyright 2021 by Philip M. Hudson.

Published 2021.

Printed in the United States of America.

All rights reserved.

No portion of this book may be reproduced, stored in a retrieval system, or transmitted in any form or by any means – electronic, mechanical, photocopy, recording, scanning, or other – except for brief quotations in critical reviews or articles, without the prior written permission of the author.

ISBN 978-1-950647-69-9

Illustrations – Google Images.

This book may be ordered from online bookstores.

Publishing Services by BookCrafters
Parker, Colorado.
www.bookcrafters.net

Table of Contents

Christmas is the Season of the Year When..1
About The Author...367
By The Author..369
What More Can I Say?...373

> Christmas is
> the season of the
> year when we believe
> that peace on earth and
> good will toward others
> actually has a pretty
> good chance of
> becoming a
> reality.

As we look around at a world that has gone mad, the gift of the Gospel of Jesus Christ provides a refuge from the uncertainties of life, and His restored Church remains an island in the storm. To those who are unsure, tentative, and hesitant, it speaks a language of stability, direction, and purpose.

Christmas
is the season
of the year when
we make room
at our inn.

As we do so, we must not be caught in the bind of building a Church while killing the articles of its faith, or permitting form to triumph over spirit. "The Church and Kingdom of God is built by the ardor and conviction of its members. We must be alert to the expansion of its assets at the cost of lost conviction. When buildings or institutions grow bigger and bigger, let us be fearful lest the Spirit will thin out." (Alvin R. Dyer).

Christmas is the
season of the year
when angels who are
the servants of Christ
are commissioned
to the work.

The office of their ministry is to call us "unto repentance, and to fulfill and to do the work of the covenants of the Father, which he hath made unto the children of men, to prepare the way by declaring the word of Christ unto the chosen vessels of the Lord, that they may bear testimony of him." (Moroni 7:31).

> Christmas is
> the season of the
> year when we learn to
> deal with the wonderful
> gift of adversity; when there
> seems to be no vacancy in the
> tightly shuttered sanctuaries
> where we would normally
> seek shelter from the
> storms of life.

When we are rebuffed by those who angrily refuse us room at the inn, we come to the realization that "tribulation for righteousness is not a blessing only, but also a gift that God giveth unto none save his special friends." (William Tyndall, "Obedience," p. 9). At the very least, when we endure such trials, we are in good company.

*Christmas
is the season of year
when we ponder the poverty
of the scene at the Manger,
and suddenly realize that
it is we who are even
less than the dust
of the earth.*

Benjamin related his "nothingness" to our debt to God and taught that if his people praised Him and served Him "with all (their) whole souls, yet (they) would be unprofitable servants." (Mosiah 2:20-21). This is because our debt to God is completely beyond our ability to pay, and we can do nothing that obliges Him to us. But He does not ask us to settle our account with Him; He asks only that we keep His commandments and regularly repent.

> Christmas is the
> season of the year when
> the promise is renewed that
> the wrong shall fail, and the
> right prevail, with peace on
> earth, and good will
> toward our fellow
> travelers.

Those who dwell in Zion are they who worship beside the manger in Bethlehem. They stand for something while Babylon's inhabitants will fall for anything. They repeatedly rededicate themselves before altars in the temple, while Babylon argues before tables in the tavern. They exist to be taught; Babylon exists to be told. They learn with their hearts; Babylon with its head. They are magnified through sacrifice; Babylon is minimized through selfishness. They assume risk, but the security of Babylon is at the expense of personal growth. Their stability is founded upon the order of the priesthood, while Babylon exists in the chaos of politics. They know that the Babe in Bethlehem promises peace, while Babylon, at best, can deliver only the absence of armed conflict.

> Christmas
> is the season
> of the year when
> shepherds of old
> remind us that the
> poor, the unlearned,
> the common person,
> and the native born,
> may equally come
> unto Christ and
> be perfected
> in Him.

Paul assured the Corinthian Saints that if they remained steadfast, in no matter what circumstances they might find themselves, no matter what cards they might have been dealt in life, in no matter what twist of fate they might think themselves trapped, ultimately, all things would be theirs, for they were "Christ's, and Christ is God's." (1 Corinthians 3:23). During the Christmas season, we Light the World with our witness of the Savior precisely because a testimony of His divinity is only dimly perceived and hesitantly believed by so many of our friends and neighbors.

Christmas is the
season of the year when our
desire to repent is intensified.
For we know that the Savior
was born to raise the sons
and daughters of earth;
born to give them
second birth.

When our lives are in harmony with Gospel principles, we are in a constant state of improvement leading to perfection. Gordon B. Hinckley testified of the blessing of faith in a world typified by the moral ambiguity of shifting values. He said: "My religion continues to teach that personal virtue is to be cherished, that honesty and integrity are central to our conduct, that civility is to be practiced, that kindness is an incumbent responsibility, and that respect for the beliefs and practices of others is a principle that cannot be avoided."

*Christmas is the
season of the year
when we recognize that
God so loved the world
that He created mistletoe.*

We need the softening influence of love before our character traits can become celestial in their nature. Love is the aether within which the qualities of heaven are captured. It bridges the gulf between its untinctured provinces and the world of everyday. In His infinite wisdom, our Father in Heaven created the mystique of mistletoe for a very special reason. (See 1 John 4:8).

Christmas
is the season
of the year when we
decorate our hearths, and
our Heavenly Father garnishes
our hearts with gentle reminders
that His Son Jesus Christ is the
Savior of the world.

When the virtue of the word of God garnishes our thoughts unceasingly, our confidence waxes strong, and the doctrine of the priesthood distils upon our heads as the dews from heaven. When our hearts are full His love, there will always remain a special place where the Holy Ghost may dwell, to be our constant companion.

Christmas is the
season of the year when
God will pour out His spirit
upon all flesh, and His sons and
His daughters will prophesy and
have dreams, and will receive
visions of fairies and enjoy
sugar plumbs dancing
about in their
heads.

"Every one that thirsteth" will come to "the waters, and he that hath no money" will "buy wine and milk without money and without price." Thus, did the prophet Isaiah exhort Israel. "Wherefore do ye spend money for that which is not bread?" he asked. "And you labour for that which satisfieth not? Hearken diligently unto me, and eat ye that which is good, and let your soul delight itself in fatness." (Isaiah 55:1-3).

Christmas is
the season of the
year when the exquisite
pattern of snowflakes
reminds us that there
is a divine design,
and that each of
us is a unique
child of
God.

It was ordained in the heavens before the world was, that we might fill the measure of our creation. Though we may be far from Home, when we feel His presence and the mystic chords of memory resonate within our heart strings, our confidence will swell and our feet will tread lightly and quickly upon the sands of time.

Christmas is the season of the year when colorful lights twinkle on fresh-fallen snow, and we see their multi-faceted reflections sparkling in the frozen crystals.

We, too, will reflect the Light when we worship the Newborn Babe. Of her mission experience in Belgium, Joanna Hudson wrote: "I'm learning that the only way I can increase my strength is to give away that which I have received. I have realized that at the end of the days when I expend the least amount of energy serving others, I am the most tired, and it is on the days when I serve my heart out that I feel rejuvenated." At an early age, Joanna had discovered how to be a prism of the Lord.

Christmas is the season of the year when it is easy to draw a contrast between the chill in the air and the warmth in our hearts.

The cold reminds us that we are "as white hot sparks struck off the divine anvil of God." (B.H. Roberts). Our flashes of faith ignite the flame of our resolve. That refiner's fire becomes a process of purification, as the dross is burned from our nature.

> Christmas
> is the season
> of the year that
> blesses us with the
> gift of energy to move
> forward with renewed
> purpose on the path
> of progress.

The Savior has given each of us tools sufficient to the task. In the light of His Gospel, we see things as they really are, and our choices are buttressed by a witness of the Spirit that comes from beyond the veil. In Him, there is "no variableness, neither shadow of turning." (James 1:17). The bedrock of His revealed word provides a more sure footing than does the uncertain and precarious path in the world of everyday that is congested with telestial traffic, raked by temporal trauma, compromised by conceptual cul-de-sacs, pockmarked by personality precipices, and damaged by doctrinal dilemmas.

> Christmas
> is the season of
> the year when we
> share the gift of
> our time, with
> others.

The Savior encouraged His disciples to focus their attention on their less fortunate brethren and to lose themselves in service. He knew that in doing so they would eventually be brought into complete harmony with the attributes of their Father in Heaven. Conforming their lives to His character traits, their nature would be transformed as they assumed both His image and His likeness. "And ye shall be even as I am," He said, "and I am even as the Father, and the Father and I are one." (3 Nephi 28:10).

> Christmas is the season of the year when, with joy, we unwrap the gift of faith.

Without it, we may have knowledge, but we will lack the power to bring about positive and lasting change. Initially, we believe what we do not see, and the reward of our faith is to see what we believe. As we gain spiritual maturity "by doing our duty, faith increases until it becomes perfect knowledge." (Heber J. Grant, C.R., 4/1934). When these qualities merge into one powerful force, the universe becomes a "machine for the making of gods." (Henri Bergson).

Christmas is
the season of the
year when the clarity
of spiritual understanding
enables us to pierce the mists
of time to see the Star that shines
brightly above a manger on the
outskirts of the little town
of Bethlehem.

Many people intellectually believe that Christ was born in Bethlehem. But their belief is nothing more than a mental assent that lacks the moral element of responsibility that we call faith. The process by which saving faith is developed is one of testing. We are taught principles and doctrine, and by obedience, blessings and power follow. Confirmation comes only after we act in faith. In this sense, "faith, if it hath not works, is dead, being alone." (James 2:17).

> Christmas
> is the season of
> the year when love
> re-establishes itself as
> the most powerful and
> persuasive force in
> the world.

"He drew a circle that left me out. Heretic, rebel, a thing to flout. But love and I had the wit to win. We scribed a circle that drew him in." (Edward Markham). God's love introduces us to "the realm of human associations, of gratitude, loyalty, and appreciation, of selflessness, helpfulness and forgiveness, of friendship, love and compassion. It is the realm of human growth and transcendence, of truth discovered and accepted, of beauty created and enjoyed, of goodness deepened and made manifest in life." (P.A. Christensen).

> Christmas
> is the season of
> the year when we
> recognize the child
> in each of us.

"The greatest tragedy in life is not children who are afraid of the dark, but men who are afraid of the light." (Plato). What a heartbreak it is to see what dies in us while we are yet alive. With child-like faith, we may say "to the man who stands at the gate of the year, 'Give me a light, that I may tread safely into the unknown.' And his reply will be: 'Go out into the darkness, and put your hand in the hand of God. That shall be to you better than a light, and safer than the known way.'" (Minnie Louise Haskins).

> Christmas is the
> season of the year when
> we realize that the love of
> our Heavenly Father that is
> expressed in the birth of His
> Son is simply beyond our
> comprehension.

God loved us so much that He gave us sweet memory, so that we might have roses in December. He loves us with the same determination that was expressed by Joseph Smith to his companions. His was a resolve "that (was) fixed, immovable, and unchangeable, to be (our) friend and brother through the grace of God in the bonds of love, to walk in all the commandments of God blameless, in thanksgiving, forever and ever." (D&C 88:133).

Christmas
is the season
of the year when
we are sustained by
our faith and our hope
during our journey to
Bethlehem to see the
Christ Child.

We "come, and adore on bended knee, Christ the Lord, the newborn King." ("Angels We Have Heard on High"). "Outwardly, God disguised him not, but made him like other men, and sent him into the world to offer himself for us a sacrifice of a sweet savour, to kill the stench of our sins, that God himself should smell them no more, nor think on them any more." (William Tyndall).

> Christmas
> is the season of the
> year when, if we remain
> alienated from the Spirit
> and far from Bethlehem,
> we must concede that
> it is we who have
> moved.

We are all "the children of (our) Father who is in heaven; (Who) maketh His sun to rise on the evil and on the good." (3 Nephi 12:45). When we sense that we are walking in shadows, it is up to us to decide whether or not we will move into the steady starlight that shines down upon the manger scene in Bethlehem.

> Christmas is
> the season of the year
> when we "choose and desire
> to be blessed with Christ in a
> little tribulation, rather than to
> be cursed perpetually with the
> world for a little pleasure."
> (William Tyndall).

We follow His admonition to turn the other cheek, to go the second mile, and to take up our cross and follow Him to Gethsemane. This is not a doctrine of passive resistance against the forces of iniquity, but of our active cooperation with powers far superior to evil. Preparation for the adversity that is a part of life endows us with the power to conquer opposition of every description and wear the laurel crown of the victor.

> Christmas is
> the season of the year
> when we feel that we have
> been caught up in coherent
> waves of the Spirit, as
> the power of heaven
> sweeps over the
> world.

When all the trappings and pretenses have been shorn away, when outward observances and phylacteries have been stripped from the ritual of our worship, when the raw sores and ugly stains of worldly influences have been healed by the Balm of Gilead, when we have given ourselves completely and without reservation to Jesus Christ, when we are without guile, and when only our true feelings remain, we can feel God's heavenly grace.

> Christmas is
> the season of the year
> when, in the midst of the
> world's turmoil, our Father
> in Heaven blesses us to
> sleep in a heavenly
> peace.

Peacemakers are "the children of God", the spiritually begotten sons and daughters of Christ who actively seek peace and are the fashioners of peace, whose behavior models the Master, who was the Prince of Peace. (3 Nephi 12:9). "Theirs is not the peace of this world, of ease, of luxury, idleness, absence of turmoil and strife, but the peace born of a righteous life, the peace that lifts the soul, that day by day brings us closer to the home of Eternal Peace, the dwelling place of our Father." (J. Reuben Clark, Jr.). Theirs is the peace that surpasses understanding, the peace that comes from obedience to Gospel principles.

> Christmas
> is the season
> of the year when,
> with heavenly angels,
> we rejoice to sing, not
> only with our voices,
> but also with our
> hearts.

Someone once facetiously observed that they regretted their inability to preach the Gospel with such power that it would result in mob violence. The point is, that in the Last Days, when the Gospel standard is measured against the shifting sands of secularism, discipleship must be lived in crescendo. As a result, the Saints will sometimes come under fire from those miscreants whose behavior is silhouetted against the shining example of the Christ child.

Christmas is
the season of the
year when, although
it may be hard for both
saints and sinners to hear
His coming, the meek will
always find room for
Him at their inn.

"We have a promise that Christ and His body and His blood and all that He did and suffered, is a sacrifice, a ransom, and a full satisfaction for our sins; that God for His sake will think no more on them, if we repent and believe." (William Tyndall).

> Christmas is
> the season of the
> year when we allow a
> little Child to lead us
> away from our bondage
> to ignorance and from
> the precipice of sin.
> (See Isaiah 11:6)

It is a season when our minds and our spirits burst from their fetters with the realization that we have been given gifts sufficient to complete our journey to the Star of David. As we move in the direction of that celestial beacon, the Savior will bless us with an awareness of our moral obligation to assist our fellow-travelers, and to introduce them to His power, that they might be lifted heavenward, as well.

Christmas
is the season of
the year when we
first hear the voice
of the Lord, muffled
as the cry of a Babe
lying in a manger,
calling us from
lands of woe.

It is a time to witness the spectacle of Babylon crumbling into dust; to realize that force and compulsion have failed miserably, as they have tried in vain to establish utopia. Peace on earth and good will "can only come through transformation of individual souls, and through lives redeemed from sin and brought in harmony with Divine will." (David O. McKay).

> Christmas is the season of the year when, for too many of God's precious children, dinner is served in a dumpster.

Before Fiorello La Guardia became mayor of New York City, he was a magistrate. One day, shortly before the Christmas holidays, there appeared before his bench a man accused of stealing a loaf of bread. Upon questioning, the man explained that he'd committed the crime to feed his starving family. Whereupon, La Guardia dismissed the case, and sentenced all present in the courtroom to pay a fine for living in a city where a man must steal to feed his wife and children.

> Christmas
> is the season of
> the year when we realize
> that His ministry will continue
> as "long as time shall last, or the
> earth shall stand, or there shall
> be one man upon the face
> thereof to be saved."
> (Moroni 7:36).

"Whosoever repenteth and cometh unto me," said the Lord, "the same is my church." (D&C 10:67-68). Since the Restoration of the Gospel on April 6, 1830, the Lord's messengers have taught this doctrine without modification. Its keystone is His grace that is extended to all who exercise saving faith on His name and enter into the straight and narrow way through the portal of baptism. (See Ether 12:26).

> Christmas is
> the season of the
> year when our Heavenly
> Father gives us the gift of
> a key that will unlock
> the mysteries of His
> Kingdom.

In wondering awe, the Christmas season has a way of adjusting our eyes to the light of the star in heaven springing, and of attuning our ears to hear the angels singing hosanna to His name. "For still is sung, in every tongue, the angels' song of glory." ("In Wondering Awe"). The mysteries of the Kingdom are the saving principles of the Gospel, designed to lead us to eternal life. They can only be discerned by the Spirit. Joseph Smith described his own experience with the mysteries in these words: "Our minds being now enlightened, we began to have the scriptures laid open to our understanding, and the true meaning and intention of their more mysterious passages revealed unto us in a manner which we never could attain to previously, nor ever before had thought of."

Christmas is the season of the year when we receive personal communication from our Heavenly Father. With a quiet cough from the manger, we are asked if we will make room for the Savior of the world to visit us during the holidays.

Revelation is a letter from God that expresses His love. "Thou hast had signs enough," Alma counseled Korihor. You "have the testimony of all these thy brethren, and also all the holy prophets. The scriptures are laid before thee, yea, and all things that are upon the face of it ... do witness that there is a Supreme Creator." (Alma 30:44). As Ralph Waldo Emerson observed: "How does nature deify us with a few and cheap elements! Give me health and a day, and I will make the pomp of emperors ridiculous."

> Christmas is the season of the year when the faithful enthusiastically prepare for the holiest of days, while a disbelieving world can see nothing but another paid holiday in its future.

We no longer put to death those who secularize His holy day, and yet we put a halt to our eternal progression and die spiritually when, as a consequence of our profane behavior, we alienate ourselves from God's influence. He created the holidays as a work-release program, and not as a vacation, for He wanted to see how we would behave when we were left on our own, after having received instruction regarding what we ought to do, which is to sing praises to His holy name. (See Alma 26:8).

> Christmas is the season of the year when, in meekness, lowliness of heart, and in humility, we follow the example of a Babe lying in the straw of a manger.

We can never show enough gratitude to Him for providing us with the gift of His prototypical example. Even though we may serve Him with all our souls, we remain unprofitable servants because our debt to Him is completely beyond our ability to pay. But rather than demanding that we settle our account with Him, He only asks that we keep His commandments, setting the stage for another Christmas gift when He blesses us even more. And so it goes; But then comes the greatest miracle of all, when we are finally redeemed by His precious blood. If we do good, and hold out faithful to the end, we will "be saved in the Kingdom of God, which is the greatest of all the gifts of God." (D&C 6:13).

Christmas
is the season of
the year when, as we
wrap our arms around
our dear friends, we
invoke the Spirit to
invite the Lamb
of God into
our hearts.

It is a time to "come up on mount Zion" to clasp hands with others and bring them into the warmth of our fellowship. We are "set to be a light unto the world, and to be the saviors of men," and so we are determined to make the journey to the Lord in the good company of our loved ones, our friends, and our neighbors. (D&C 103:9, see Obadiah 1:21).

Christmas is the
season of the year
when we recognize that
Heavenly Father has exalted
His Son, and has "given him
a name which is above
every (other) name."
(Philippians 2:9).

"For unto us a child is born, unto us a son is given; and the government shall be upon his shoulder: and his name shall be called Wonderful, Counselor, the mighty God, the everlasting Father, the Prince of Peace." (Isaiah 9:6). The Savior earned all these titles "because of the glory His Father had given Him before He was born, and because at that time He was already God." (Joseph Smith).

Christmas is the season of the year when we paw through the telestial trinkets that have been piled beneath the tree, and to our dismay realize that batteries are not included. For that power, we need look no further than to the Babe of Bethlehem.

Wrote the poet: "My day-old child lay in my arms. With my lips against his ear, I whispered strongly, 'How I wish that you could hear. I've a hundred wonderful things to say. (A tiny cough and a nod). Hurry, and grow, so I can tell you about God.' My day-old baby's mouth was still, and my words only tickled his ear. But a kind of a light passed through his eyes, and I saw this thought appear: 'How I wish I had a voice, and words. I've a hundred things to say. Before I forget, I'd tell you of God. I only left Him yesterday.'" (Carol Lynn Pearson, "Day Old Child"). How wonderful must the resurrected Savior have felt, when He revealed to Joseph Smith: "Verily, I say unto you, that as many as receive me, to them will I give power to become the sons of God." (D&C 11:30).

> Christmas is
> the season of the
> year when families
> should be home for
> the holidays, but
> too frequently
> are not.

"There's no place like home for the holidays, 'cause no matter how far away you roam, if you wanna be happy in a million ways, when you pine for the sunshine of a friendly gaze, for the holidays you can't beat home sweet home!" (Al Stillman & Robert Allen, "Home For The Holidays"). Wherever we may be during the Christmas season, our membership in the Church and Kingdom guarantees that we will be "no more strangers and foreigners, but fellow citizens with the Saints, and of the household of God." (Ephesians 2:19).

Christmas is the season of the year when our immersion in the fiery element of the Spirit becomes the crucible in which we burn.

Our celebration of Christmas every twelve months helps to recalibrate our moral compass. The celestial standard that is set by the story of the Christ Child softens the trauma we have all experienced as a result of our having been dumped somewhat unceremoniously onto the world stage.

> Christmas is the season of the year when many realize that they are only living after the manner of happiness. It was to them, in particular, that Moroni extended the invitation to come unto Christ and be perfected in Him. (See Moroni 10:30).

For those who take pleasure in sin, both their understanding and their behavior harmonize with worldly standards. As long as they can shut out the light of Christ, they may live under the illusion that they are happy. But sooner or later, the discrepancy between their marginalized behavior and Gospel ideals will become so great that their short-lived pleasure in their worldly ways will be destroyed by the realization that their experiences were counterfeit, and that wickedness never was happiness. Christmas is an invitation from God to come in from the cold of their self-induced alienation from the Spirit.

Christmas is the season of the year when the voice of angels once more proclaims: "Glory to God in the highest, and on earth, peace, good will toward men." (Luke 2:14). That glad message is heard far more clearly than any tumult of opinion or war of words.

"I see the stars; I hear the rolling thunder; thy power throughout the universe displayed. Then sings my soul, my Savior God, to Thee, How great Thou art." ("How Great Thou Art"). A glorious morning is breaking for the people of His choice, who retreat from the world, and for a defense set watchmen on their walls to loudly proclaim that the Son of God is born this Christmas Day.

> Christmas is the
> season of the year
> when we can see
> in its symbols
> the gifts of
> God.

Our receipt of these gifts is "inseparably connected to the powers of heaven, and ... the powers of heaven cannot be controlled nor handled only upon the principles of righteousness." (D&C 121:36). Happy are those who discover the power of Christmas, "for the merchandise of it is better than the merchandise of silver, and the gain thereof than fine gold. (It) is more precious than rubies." (Proverbs 3:13-15). Any gifts that we might find beneath the tree pale in comparison to those which God has given us.

Christmas
is the season
of the year when the
frenzied commotion of
commerce is contrasted
with the quiet reflection
that occurs away in a
manger, far from the
madding crowds
at shopping
malls.

Our observance of Christmas is a strengthening exercise for our spiritual core. The season will take on new meaning, empowering us to cry out: "Blessed be the name of He that cometh in the name of the Lord; Thou art my God and I will bless Thee; Thou art my God and I will exalt Thee." (Psalms 118:28).

> Christmas is
> the season of the
> year when we look at
> shiny ornaments, and
> see a reflection that
> is a representation
> of the full stature
> of our spirits.

Because of the Savior of the world, in the resurrection, "all deformities and imperfections will be removed, and the body will conform to the likeness of the spirit." (Joseph Fielding Smith, Jr.). Joseph F. Smith said: "From the day of the resurrection, the body will develop until it reaches the full measure of the stature of its spirit." ("Gospel Doctrine," p. 23). In the Christ Child, we see the purity of the spirit that we all possessed when we came into the world. As we grow older, the incessant wave action of the world lapping at our spiritual footings may undermine our power grid and cause us to lose the intrinsic light with which our Heavenly Father has blessed us. Christmas can be a gentle reminder to nurture the light that glows from within.

Christmas is the
season of the year
when the potential of
children gives us hope
that by small things
the world can be
changed.

Carl Sandburg was thinking of Abraham Lincoln, but it could have been the Savior, when he wrote: "Not often in the story of mankind does a man arrive on earth who is both steel and velvet, who is hard as rock and soft as a drifting fog, who holds in his heart and mind the paradox of terrible storm and peace unspeakable and perfect." The Savior's example invites us to conquer the natural man and harness the power within us; to become submissive, even as little children, so that our true potential for greatness may be revealed.

Christmas is the season of the year when doubt and hesitancy yield to unbridled optimism and enthusiasm.

A young missionary who had caught the vision and had incredible enthusiasm for the work was assigned by his mission president to be the senior companion of an elder who could not get along with others because of his negative outlook on life. After a couple of weeks, the mission president called his dynamic young Elder and asked him how things were going. "Fantastic!" he replied. "Elder Brown and I have discovered we have something in common." "What's that?" asked his surprised president. Replied the Elder, "Neither one of us has ever been to Africa!"

> Christmas
> is the season of the
> year when we look at the
> scene in the Manger, and
> realize that we, too, may
> increase "in wisdom
> and stature, and in
> favor with God."
> (Luke 2:52).

"Come, follow me," said the Lord, Who then gave the all-encompassing and mind-expanding command to be perfect, even as He and His Father were perfect. Thus, did the Lord reveal that it is our destiny to develop both the image and the likeness of our Heavenly Father; to become a reflection of both His countenance and His character.

Christmas is the season of the year when presidents, magistrates, potentates, powers, and principalities pale in comparison to the government of God that would be led by the Newborn King.

When we learn to govern ourselves in harmony with the laws of heaven, we will be moving forward on the path leading to God's Kingdom. Then, when we finally stand before Him to render an accounting, we will realize that He was always on our side, while Satan, the great detractor, was always in opposition. At that moment, we will realize that ours had always been the deciding vote. Perhaps the Kingdom of God can be both a theocracy and a democracy, after all.

> Christmas is the season of the year when "I" and "Mine" more easily yield to "Thee" and "Thine".

Our commemoration of the birth of the Savior helps us to deal with our pronoun problem; to think more in terms of "thyself" than "myself". It helps us to overcome the conundrum of our misplaced fealty that can build to a climax during the crazy shopping season between Thanksgiving, a holiday whose name is becoming increasingly ironic, and Chritma, a holy day that is becoming increasingly secularized.

Christmas is the season of the year when the sweeping panorama of Heavenly Father's divine design intuitively makes more sense, and more easily unfolds to our view.

The glittering facets of the Spirit allow us to see beyond the limited horizon of our natural vision. When John Widtsoe traveled to England, the immigration official who interviewed him, said: "If I were to let you enter Britain, what would you teach our people?" Elder Witdsoe said: "I would teach them where they came from, why they are here, and where they are going." The official looked up at him, and asked: "Does your church teach that?" Elder Witdsoe replied: "It does." "Well mine doesn't," he responded, and he came down with his stamp on the passport, signed it, and said: "You may enter!"

> Christmas
> is the season
> of the year when
> "a tale as old as time,
> and as true as it can be"
> speaks to us from the
> dust. ("Beauty and
> The Beast").

There is an interesting account of the discovery of the Bar Kokhba Documents that were hidden in caves near Ein Gedi on the western shore of the Salt Sea, in the second century, A.D. These records were deliberately buried deeply in the dry earth of the cave floor, and when they came to light there were choking clouds of dust, so that the archaeologists had to wear masks in order to breathe. Truly, the voices of the prophets that testify of the birth of Christ "speak out of the ground," their speech is "low out of the dust," and they "whisper out of the dust." (Isaiah 29:4).

Christmas
is the season of the
year when we lift up our
"voices in song and in story,"
to "let banners of peace in
all lands be unfurled."
("Awake and Arise").

Negotiators may sue for peace while antagonists try to gain the advantage, but there will be no peace in the world until every faction acknowledges the supremacy of the Prince of Peace.

Christmas is the season of the year when we remember that the earth "was once a garden place, with all her glories common, and men did live a holy race, and worship Jesus face to face, in Adam-ondi-Ahman." ("Adam-ondi-Ahman").

When clouds of apostasy benight the minds of men, confusion arises concerning the doctrines of the Kingdom and the simplest policies and procedures of the Church, and there can be no enlightened solution to the problem. Only the direct intervention of Heavenly Father and His Son Jesus Christ can banish the darkness. They intervene from the heavens with thunderous voices, blazing visions, and brightly burning stars in the east. (See Matthew 2:2).

> Christmas
> is the season of the
> year when the world itself
> reawakens. Mists of darkness
> evaporate, as does a wil-
> of-the-wisp, in the
> light of day.

When our appetites spin wildly out of control, our passions forge our fetters. At that moment, our birthright is sold for a mess of pottage, for we have made a compact with the devil. The Savior came to break these bands. (See Mosiah 15:9). Even though there may now be almost universal commotion from ocean to ocean, the events of that Christmas morning herald the dawn of a beautifully bright new day.

Christmas
is the season of the
year when those who have
been inspired from heaven
are sent to "stand among the
people in all the land," and
to awaken in their hearts
gratitude to God for the
gift of His newborn Son.
(3 Nephi 6:20).

With gratitude, we pray "that we might toil, and not seek for rest; that we might give and not count the cost; that we might fight, and not heed the wounds; and that we might labor, and not ask for any reward, save that of knowing that we do God's will." (Ignatius Loyola).

Christmas
is the season of
the year when we recall
that it was "in the beauty of
the lilies, that Christ was born
across the sea, with a glory in his
bosom that transfigures you and me."
("Battle Hymn of The Republic").

The work of the ministry of the Savior is to transform us. He will carry us along as far as we need to go, gently lifting us higher and higher, until we reach the summit of our own Mount of Transfiguration. At that day, our faces will shine, and our raiment will be as bright as the rays of the sun.

Christmas is
the season of the
year when we realize
that the pathway leading
to the Kingdom of Heaven
does not only pass through
Bethlehem. It also winds its
way to an empty tomb by
way of the Garden of
Gethsemane and
Calvary.

When we finally arrive at heaven's gate, its keeper will not be Saint Peter, but the Lord Himself, for "he employeth no servant there." (2 Nephi 9:41). As it was for Alma and his people, so will be for us. His word will have become our Liahona. By following His compass, we will have found that no wind could blow so hard except it filled our sails. Although we may have tacked many times on a voyage that was fraught with storms, and were menaced again and again by hidden reefs, and though we may have tarried at intermediate ports-of-call along the way, our final destination was always sure.

Christmas
is the season of the
year when we not only
wear our Sunday finery,
but we also put on our best
behavior. We realize that our
outward appearance mirrors
our inner self. It dawns on
us that the acorn doesn't
fall far from the tree,
and that we might
yet grow into a
mighty oak.

Alma asked the people of Zarahemla: "Have ye spiritually been born of God? Have ye received His image in your countenances? Have ye experienced this mighty change in your heart?" (Alma 5:14). And then came the more penetrating question, posed a few verses later: "And now ... if ye have experienced a change of heart, and if ye have felt to sing the song of redeeming love, I would ask, can ye feel so now?" (Alma 5:26).

Christmas
is the season of the
year that was designed by
God to give both saints and
sinners alike an opportunity
to pause and reflect upon
the meaning and the
purpose of their
lives.

"How silently, how silently, the wondrous gift is given; so God imparts to human hearts the blessings of His heaven." ("O Little Town of Bethlehem"). We realize that God has given us "a sheet of paper white, where each of us may write a line or two, and then comes night. Greatly begin. If thou hast time but for a line, make that sublime. Not failure, but low aim is crime." (James Lowell).

*Christmas
is the season
of the year when the
heavens smile down upon
us, because stewardship and
consecration have so easily
come together to enjoy
perfect symmetry.*

John K. Edmunds had a distinguished legal career. One day a widow came to him for advice, and when they were finished, she apprehensively asked, "How much do I owe you?" Gently, he replied, "Why don't you pay me what you think it is worth." Relieved, she got out her coin purse, produced a quarter, and pressed it into his hand. He looked at the quarter, looked at her, and then got out his own coin purse, and gave her ten cents change.

> Christmas is the season of the year when we yield to the better angels of our nature and trust in what we learned aeons ago.

"Religious recognition is just that; a re-cognition; a re-knowing; the sum of existence. If we thwart or suppress that instinctive response, we are accountable, and to a degree, we condemn ourselves. We knew Christ before this life, we know Him here, and we will know Him hereafter." (Truman Madsen). How Christmas touches us can deify us or destroy us. It is a story with many layers of meaning that can unfold for us, as it did for Him.

Christmas is the
season of the year
when we resolve to be
more than only Christians
of Convenience who lack the
burning fire that is shut up in
the bones of His disciples.
(See Jeremiah 20:9).

There is a perpetual battle raging in our hearts, pitting our desire to serve our Master against telestial tendencies that twist our focus inward. "Two ways always lie open before us, one leading to an ever-lower plane, where are heard the cries of despair and the curses of the poor; and the other leading to the highlands of the morning, where are heard the glad shouts of humanity, and where honest effort is rewarded with immortality." (John P. Altgeld).

Christmas is the season of the year when a chorus of voices shouting "Hallelujah" is lifted heavenward, hastening the millennial reign of the Lord.

When we participate in the "Hosanna Shout", we stand upon our feet and strike our right hand into the palm of our left hand at the end of each word, sometimes adding the words "forever and ever, worlds without end" following the regular words "to God and the Lamb." Since 1893, we wave white handkerchiefs during the Shout. Afterwards, we might sing a hymn. But with these different modifications that have been introduced from time to time, the basic pattern of "The Hosanna Shout", repeated three times while waving white handkerchiefs, has persisted to the present day.

> Christmas
> is the season of the
> year when we reach out
> to those whose hearts beat
> to the discordant rhythm
> of sounding brass and
> tinkling cymbals.

If we "hinder a very infidel from the right of that law, we sinneth against God." (William Tyndall, "Obedience" p. 61). With profound gratitude for His generosity, we extend the hand of fellowship to others, regardless of their circumstances in life. "And it shall come to pass that ye shall divide (the land) by lot for an inheritance unto you, and to the strangers that sojourn among you, which shall beget children among you; and they shall be unto you as born in the country among the children of Israel; they shall have inheritance with you among the tribes of Israel." (Ezekiel 47:22).

Christmas
is the season of
the year when visions
of sugar plumbs that look
an awful lot like cash bonuses
dance in our heads, threatening
to crowd out our gratitude for
the best performance-related
gift of all, which is to enter
into the joy of the Lord.

Those who determine to follow in the footsteps of the Savior are like "brave Horatius, the Captain of the Gate," who declared: "To each of us upon this earth, death cometh soon or late. And how can we die better than facing fearful odds, for the ashes of our fathers, and the temples of our gods?" ("Lays of Ancient Rome," Thomas Babbington Macaulay).

> Christmas is the season of the year when we wisely learn to manage the tension that is a part of our everyday lives.

We are anxiously engaged in good causes and do many things of our own free will, and thus we bring to pass much righteousness. We are agents unto ourselves, and the power is in us to deal constructively with stress and channel it into an influence for good. (See D&C 58:27-28).

Christmas is the
season of the year when
laughter in the air catalyzes the
commitment of gentle men and women
everywhere to let nothing dismay them
from seeking God's rest. With joy,
they remember that Jesus Christ
their Savior was born on
Christmas Day.

Our impenetrable shield of faith allows us to more easily identify and deal with Satan's fingerprints on the idols with which he tempts us. Eternal perspective allows us to discern between happiness and its worldly counterfeits, and other polarized opposites. We persevere, because "there's no time like the present; no present like time, and life can be over in the space of a rhyme." (Georgia Byng).

Christmas is the season of the year when many pause to reflect upon their circumstances, and suffer the mental anguish that comes with their recognition of dashed hopes and lost opportunities.

"But you were always a good man of business, Jacob," said Scrooge. "Business!" cried the ghost, wringing its hands. "Mankind was my business. The common welfare was my business; charity, mercy, forbearance, and benevolence were all my business. The dealings of my trade were but a drop of water in the comprehensive ocean of my business." (Charles Dickens, "A Christmas Carol").

Christmas is the season of year when the pure innocence of the Babe lying in the manger stands in sharp contrast to the guilt and pain of unresolved sin.

Sin can be "like an unquenchable fire" that leaves our hope for happiness in ashes. (Mosiah 2:38). David O. McKay taught: "The first condition of happiness is a clear conscience." ("Gospel Ideals," p. 498). In physical terms, before a wound can heal, it has to be clean. The same principle applies to character development. A noble character has no festering sores or skeletons lurking in the closet. The gift of recurring repentance releases us from our bondage to sin, unleashes the powers of heaven in our behalf, and qualifies us by worthiness to enjoy the blessings reserved for the faithful. Heavenly Father's Only Begotten Son makes it possible for us to overcome our limitations and reach our potential. It is by conforming our lives to His celestial standard that the bands of death are broken and our spiritual transformation is made possible.

> Christmas is the
> season of the year
> when we remember
> His Apostles
> of old.

These inspired men "brought forth the key of the sweet promises, saying, repent, and be baptized every one of you in the name of Jesus Christ for the remission of sins, and ye shall receive the gift of the Holy Ghost." (William Tyndall, "Obedience" p. 66). Many find it easy to follow their counsel so long as it takes them on to sprawling avenues dotted with conveniently located rest stops, and to brightly lighted world stages filled with the appreciative applause and laudatory comments of supportive audiences. But placed in challenging situations with no-one looking, when there have been no preparatory fortifying experiences and there are no positive peer pressures to sustain correct choices, it is far easier to falter.

> Christmas is
> the season of the year
> when the vision of a Babe
> lying in a manger helps each
> of us to return to the secret
> garden of our childhood,
> where the spiritual roots
> of our relationships
> first received the
> tender nurture
> of God.

Our foundation for happiness is based on the common bonds of spiritual interdependency. The links thus forged emphasize the power of the ordinances of the Gospel to unite families and make life sublime. The Savior taught: "Abundance is multiplied unto (the Saints) through the manifestations of the Spirit." (D&C 70:13). Eternal objectives stay in focus when we measure our progress against the spiritual footings of family relationships.

> Christmas is the
> season of the year when
> purposeful preparation
> is put in proper
> perspective.

The Christmas season is a good time for us to prepare to meet God; to perform our labors, to have the soul scars of sin healed through repentance, and to allow the Spirit to groom us for a glorious resurrection and reunion with our loved ones in His Celestial Kingdom. (See Alma 34:32).

Christmas
is the season of
year when it is easy
to relate to Santa's elves,
who have doubtless been
toiling non-stop at his
workshop near the
North Pole.

Although we are and will forever be God's junior partners, His "elves" and never His equals, we still know what it feels like to be in business with Him. When we work hard and the sweat drips off the ends of our noses, we thank Him for whatever talents and energy we may have been given to apply to our capacity to work. When we survey the fruits of our labor, we try to envision the greater purpose for which our blessings have come. We try to be good stewards, and if our talents are multiplied, our greatest enjoyment comes when they are put to use for the benefit of others.

> Christmas
> is the season of
> the year when crisp
> winter air helps us to
> see more clearly the
> obstacles to our
> progression.

The first enemy we will encounter "is within ourselves. It is a good thing to overcome that enemy first, and bring ourselves into strict obedience to the principles of life and salvation which He has given to the world for our salvation." (Joseph F. Smith, C.R., 10/1914). The apostle Paul's formula for ridding ourselves of the past was "forgetting those things which are behind, and reaching forth unto those things which are before." (Philippians 3:13-14). When we take his advice, we find ourselves anticipating Christmas with new-found enthusiasm.

> Christmas
> is the season
> of the year when
> we find ourselves
> bathed in the light
> of truth, in all
> its stunning
> clarity.

As we are taught by the Spirit, we stare in wide-eyed wonder at the beautiful simplicity of the interwoven threads within the fabric of the pattern of Gospel principles that makes up the tapestry of The Plan of Salvation. We respond to the invitation to come unto Christ in a very simple and uncomplicated way. We "ask with a sincere heart, with real intent, having faith in Christ." (Moroni 10:4). We "ask in faith, nothing wavering." (James 1:6).

> Christmas is the
> season of the year
> when we all try a little
> harder to be grateful,
> smart, clean, true,
> prayerful, and
> humble.

We are profoundly influenced by the virtue of the Christ Child, and our "delight is in the law of the Lord; and in (it we) mediate day and night." (Psalms 1:2). Our spiritual maturity allows us to follow general principles and scriptural guidelines, listen to the promptings of the Spirit, and ask: "Are my actions holy and of service to God? Am I doing good? Am I using my agency to keep myself unspotted from the world? Am I honoring the Lord as one of His true disciples? Am I keeping Christ in Christmas?"

> Christmas is the
> season of the year
> that can breathe new
> life into the body
> of believers and
> non-believers
> alike.

Christmas is designed to penetrate hearts, heal deafness and blindness, and ease the tension and inelasticity that too often characterize our attitudes, so that "when we are dead, others will seek our tombs, not in the earth, but in what had been in our hearts." (Jalal al Din al Rumi, the 14th century Sufi poet who founded the Order of Dervishes). Its sweet fragrance smells like bread that is fresh out of the oven. The supremacy of its spiritual certainty is unhindered by the limitations of material ambiguity that jostle for our attention. It encourages us to work behind the scenes without pay and far from media attention. It asks us to assume the roles of secret elves who leave plates of cookies on doorsteps, ring the bell, and run.

> Christmas is
> the season of the year
> when we raise our eyes
> above the far horizon
> of time, to see the
> Lord through His
> redeeming
> love.

"Someone once said that time is a predator that stalks us all our lives. I prefer to think of it as a companion that accompanies us on the journey, reminding us to cherish every moment." (Captain Jean Luc Picard, "Star Trek - The Next Generation"). The Savior teaches us how to manipulate time; to give it, take it, spend it, find it, and buy it, while hopefully not killing it. God gave us the gift of the precious commodity of time to give us enough latitude to make regular deposits to our spiritual bank accounts.

> Christmas is
> the season of the
> year when too many
> trivialize the celestial,
> secularize the sacred,
> and set at naught
> the Savior of
> the world.

We recall how the Savior scattered the tables of the money changers at the temple, and it strikes us how cheaply "for which all virtue is sold, and almost any vice – almighty gold!" (Ben Jonson). The irony is that it is all for nothing; a passion for telestial trash can result in fratricidal bickering and "the destruction of nearly all the people of the kingdom." (Ether 9:12).

> Christmas
> is the season
> of the year when the
> Word of God, like a two
> edged sword, separates
> truth from error, and
> strikes terror in the
> hearts of the
> wicked.

And yet, the faithful still pray for those who refuse to believe and who find fault with our celebration of the birth of the Savior. We remember William Tyndale's gentle counsel: "For what praise is it, when ye be buffeted for your faults, ye take it patiently? But when ye do well, and ye suffer wrong and take it patiently, then is there thanks with God. Hereunto verily were ye called." Ultimately, "we can never be injured by any mortals, except ourselves." (Heber J. Grant, C.R., 4/1909).

> Christmas is the season of the year when it just seems to be more natural for us to obey the Golden Rule.

"When thou hurtest not thy neighbours, then art thou sure that God's Spirit worketh in thee and that thy faith is no dream nor any false imagination." (William Tyndall, "Obedience" p. 54). "Blessed are the merciful," the Savior taught, "for they shall obtain mercy." (3 Nephi 12:7). "For with what judgment ye judge, ye shall be judged: and with what measure ye mete, it shall be measured to you again." (Matthew 7:2). What goes around comes around, and if you cast your bread upon the waters, after many days it shall return to you. (See Ecclesiastes 11:1).

> Christmas is
> the season of the
> year when we realize
> that one of Heavenly
> Father's greatest gifts
> to His children is the
> happiness that is the
> companion of an
> untroubled
> soul.

We choose the Holy Child of Bethlehem in an act of free will that yields our hearts to Him. We ponder the great and terrible consequences of Gethsemane, travel with Him to Calvary, and enjoy the sweetness of the redeeming power of the Atonement. When we keep His laws, we experience the "happiness which is prepared for the saints" that will transcend temporal insecurity and discomfort, and neutralize the pathetic passion for pleasure that is the worldly counterfeit to joy. (2 Nephi 9:43). We are not alone, now or ever. This is one of the gifts we receive at Christmas.

> Christmas
> is the season
> of the year when we
> soberly remember that it
> was among the poor, the
> mean, and the lowly,
> that our Savior
> lived.

Perhaps the circumstances of His birth and the unpretentious lifestyle of His family contributed to His intolerance of the Pharisees of His own day, hypocrites who pretended to be pious when they were only going through the motions. With the Pharisees, we are free to follow one lifestyle or the other, but not both. That desire runs counter to the laws of nature and is fatally flawed. Christmas is God's remedy for those who are traveling down a one-way road toward a personality precipice overlooking the gates of hell. (See Matthew 9:12).

Christmas is the season of the year when we recall how silently the wondrous gift was given, as "God imparted to human hearts, the blessings of his heaven." ("O Little Town of Bethlehem").

Is it too much for Him to ask us to forgive each other? Without it, The Merciful Plan of the Great Creator can redeem neither those who are on the "giving end" nor on the "receiving end" of injury. The example of Christ's Atonement requires forgiveness by both parties; by all who would be obedient to the Laws of the Celestial Kingdom. With laconic humor, Brigham Young declared: "He who takes offense when none was intended is a fool, and he who takes offense when one was intended is usually a fool."

Christmas is the season of the year when we beg: "Be near me, Lord Jesus. I ask thee to stay close by me forever, and love me, I pray." ("Away in a Manger").

When we are drawn to the Savior, our charity becomes a tacit acknowledgement that we really do know Him, that His teachings mean everything to us, and that we are close enough to Him to be brought under the spell of His compassion for the world.

> Christmas is the season of the year when we dolefully remember that much of what we do in this life, we do for ourselves.

At the same time, we understand that God "overcame us with kindness and to make us to do of very love that thing which the law compels us to do. For love only and to do service unto our neighbors is the fulfilling of the law in the sight of God." (William Tyndall). When our altruistic sensitivities predominate, we labor in behalf of others and lose ourselves in service. When we have caught the vision and because of our implicit trust in Him, we give ourselves to the Savior by yielding to Him our agency.

Christmas is the
season of the year that
teaches when God wants to
change the world, He needs only
to bring one of His precious little
ones into the nurturing arms of
a mother. Then, He lets her
take over, and do the
rest.

"And she brought forth her first-born son, and wrapped him in swaddling clothes, and laid him in a manger: because there was no room for them in the inn." (Luke 2:7). "And the child grew, and waxed strong in spirit, filled with wisdom; and the grace of God was upon him." (Luke 2:40).

> Christmas is the season of the year when we see in vision the Banquet of Consequences; and we hope that it will be as inviting as a turkey with all the trimmings.

The eternities are not focused, as we so often are, on a desperate scramble for scarce resources. Even now, there is enough, and to spare. The Lord has promised us the fullness of the earth. Yea, all things which come of the earth, in the season thereof, are made for the benefit and the use of man, both to please the eye and to gladden the heart; Yea, for food and for raiment, for taste and for smell, to strengthen the body and to enliven the soul." (D&C 59:15-19).

> Christmas
> is the season of the
> year when the universal
> language of laughter fills
> the air, and engaging smiles
> penetrate borders and tear
> down boundaries.

When we feel happy, we smile with all our heart, and when we're down, we smile with all our might. If we do nothing else, we can still be the smile on the faces of those who mourn or stand in need of comfort. Our smiles can be a daily exercise that we can do without ever breaking a sweat. The smiles that we wear on the outside tell others what's happening on the inside. Our joy may be the source of our smile, but sometimes our smile may be the source of our joy. As we smile with a determined effort to fight our way through brimming tears, we can take comfort in the fact that at least the corners of our mouths point toward heaven. When we get up in the morning, we are only half-dressed until we put on our smile. We realize that, when it comes to smiling, one size fits all. Our smile is an accessory who never goes out of style.

> Christmas is the season of the year when we are reminded that the Savior is the Great I Am. For better or for worse, He is our Father's gift to us, and He remains a silent witness to our thoughts, our words, and our deeds.

If our hearts are right, "then we (will) have confidence toward God. And whatsoever we ask, we (will) receive of him, because we keep his commandments, and do those things that are pleasing in his sight." (1 John 3:21-22). Truly, "we should believe on the name of his Son Jesus Christ, and love one another." (1 James 3:23). The Savior knew that in the world in which we live the distinctions between good and evil would be blurred. Spiritual Babylon is all around us, and so we need to be vigilant because "vice is a monster of so frightful mien, as to be hated needs but to be seen. Yet seen too oft, familiar with her face, we first endure, then pity, then embrace." (Alexander Pope). We must recognize virtue when we see it, and cleave unto every good thing at Christmas time and throughout the year.

> Christmas is the season of the
> year when we are given the gift of
> independence, with an opportunity to
> reprioritize our objectives and to
> recalibrate our moral compass
> while bathed in the light that
> has been provided by the
> Star of Bethlehem.

Unlike indulgent parents, our Heavenly Father will not give us that which we don't deserve, nor will He generally respond to our pressure to give us that which we do not need. Instead, He has promised a great endowment and blessing of spiritual and priesthood power to be poured out upon us, inasmuch as we are faithful and continue in humility before Him. (See D&C 105:112). Progress depends upon how we handle our free will, in the sense that we do not allow it to turn on us and lead us into temptation. Instead, we must use it as a tool to deliver us from evil. It can be our greatest friend and benefactor, especially if we re-enthrone the Savior as the reason for the season.

Christmas is the
season of the year when
the Spirit confirms to us that
our opportunity for happiness is a
wonderful gift from our Father in
Heaven that has been woven under
His direction into the fabric of
every Gospel principle.

Even though "dark threads are as needful in the weaver's skillful hand as the threads of gold and silver, in the pattern he has planned," (Benjamin Malachi Franklin), when we accept the invitation to "try the virtue of the word of God," its fabric will introduce us to the fruit of the Tree of Life. Our senses will embrace the matchless realm of joy available only through obedience to Gospel principles. (Alma 31:5).

Christmas is the season
of the year when we can only
imagine the divine fervor of the
Christ Child, and the sparkle in
His eyes that presaged the
unbridled enthusiasm
of His youth.

When we are tempted to be a bit self-righteous and think that we are worthy of our fame and fortune, let us remember that they are as "a vapor, and popularity is an accident, and those who cheer you today may curse you tomorrow. In the end, the only thing that endures is character." (Attributed to Horace Greely) We determine to focus upon the unlimited potential of the divine model, that is found not only in the Christ Child, but also in every precious baby who comes into the world.

> Christmas is the season of the year that infuses us with the resolve to be valiant in our testimony of Jesus.

It is within the milieu of the dazzling light that attended the birth of the Savior that we work out our salvation with fear and trembling before Him. (See Philippians 2:12). As we daily confront assaults on our spiritual solidarity, we try to remember that, in every case, our Heavenly Father will weigh in on one side of the scale, and the counterfeit coin of Satan's spurious currency will clatter down in a cacophony of confusion on the other side of the scale. Our destiny hangs in the balance, and ultimately, on every issue there are three votes cast. Heavenly Father casts His vote in favor of us, and Satan bets against us. As all eternity holds its collective breath, we cast the deciding vote.

> Christmas is the
> season of the year when
> our thoughts turn to the
> Father of Lights, Who
> gave the Greatest
> Gift of all.

Our gratitude to our Heavenly Father is deeper than thanks. Thankfulness is the beginning of gratitude and may consist merely of words, but gratitude is shown in action. Our gratitude displays its true colors at Christmas time, when it urges us on to perform random acts of kindness.

Christmas is the season of the year that touches the mystic chords of our memory so that we might recognize both the brotherhood of mankind and the fatherhood of God. We understand how His Firstborn Son is our Exemplar, the Good Shepherd, our Advocate, Mediator, and the Bread of Life.

He is the tangible and effectual bridge between the secular and the sacred. Christmas is a great time to remember that the differences between us matter very little. Saints and sinners are very much alike, after all. When the Savior was born of Mary at Bethlehem, He leveled the playing field and we lost the right to attach labels to others.

> Christmas is the season
> of the year when the star above
> Bethlehem blesses the world with a
> heavenly beacon for all to follow
> without regard to their station
> in life. It reminds us that
> wise men still seek Him
> that was born King
> of the Jews.

Mortality has been designed as a life-long learning laboratory that would give us the opportunity to mold our nature to more closely resemble that of our Father in Heaven. Our freedom to choose in an atmosphere so full of dangerous deceptions, enticing entrapments, perilous pathways, and soothing seductions entails great risk. There are, however, places of refuge and times of the year that are untainted from the blood and sins of our generation, where we may flee from Spiritual Babylon to shelter our spirits, quiet our racing hearts, ease the tensions that build up when we spend too much time in the fast lane of life, grasp the horns of sanctuary, and quietly reflect on the quality of our preparation to live with Heavenly Father for eternity.

Christmas
is the season of the
year when we visualize the
quiet scene in the manger and
realize that the story that never
grows old is the catalyst that
propels us on a quest to
discover the divine
source of our
being.

It is not enough that we know about His birth, by reading in Luke, or by listening to others speak of Him. We must know Him through the bonds of common experience and feeling. Our religion is more involved with recovery than discovery. Our destiny is not union, but reunion with divine realities. Our religious recognition is a re-acquaintance with that which we have already learned. We are reminded of Dag Hammarskjöld's observation: "The longest journey is the journey inward, for he who has chosen his destiny has started upon a quest for the source of his being."

> Christmas is the season of
> the year that teaches to us find
> joy in the world, even as we paw
> our way through sounding brass
> and tinkling cymbals that
> have been gift wrapped
> and placed under
> the tree.

It is very difficult to tell just what brings us happiness. Both poverty and wealth have failed miserably. Neither fame nor anonymity holds the key. Both principalities and the absence of worldly influence are inadequate. Neither beauty nor the beast has the advantage. However, inspired men have revealed this much, that "happiness is the object and design of our existence and will be the end thereof if we pursue the path that leads to it." (Joseph Smith). The gift that Jesus Christ gives to us each Christmas season is light to illuminate our path toward His example of virtue, uprightness, faithfulness, holiness, and keeping all of the commandments of God.

Christmas is the season of the year when the concerns of the world become less significant and progressively transparent.

Our celebration of the birth of Jesus Christ gives us the opportunity to set aside the concerns that seem to occupy our attention for so much of the rest of the year, when we "tend to fill space, as if what we have, what we are, is not enough. Being affluent, we strangle ourselves with what we can buy, things whose ambiguity obstructs our ability to see what is really there." (Gretel Erlich).

Christmas is
the season of the year
when we remember that, as
the Babe grew in wisdom and
stature, He "needed not that
any man should teach him."
(J.S.T. Matthew 3:24).

Maybe we are not born an empty tablet upon which we write with the chalk of childhood. Maybe, as did the Christ Child, we have "swift, untinctured affinity and response to our own burning deeps; a whole, happy, healthy relationship with the core of creativity and spirituality." (Truman Madsen).

Christmas
is the season
of the year when we
respond to the invitation
to make room in our
hearts for the love
of God.

Epictetus, writing in Rome at about the same time as the birth of the Savior, observed: "The universe is but one great city, full of beloved ones, divine and human, by nature endeared to each other." Later, after the ministry of the Savior among the Nephites, their love was so great that Mormon was moved to declare: "Surely there could not be a happier people among all the people who had been created by the hand of God." (4 Nephi 1:15-16).

> Christmas
> is the season
> of the year when
> we experience the
> spiritual hunger of
> the obediently
> faithful.

We emulate those who pressed "forward with a steadfastness in Christ" who exhibited child-like faith. (2 Nephi 31:20). Christmas gives us time to reflect upon the fact that "the earth rolls upon her wings, and the sun giveth his light by day, and the moon giveth her light by night, and the stars also give their light, as they roll upon their wings in their glory, in the midst of the power of God." (D&C 88:45).

Christmas is
the season of the year
when God places His infant
Son squarely in the cross-hairs
to capture the world's attention. The
story has persisted, that each year, we
might once again come and adore Him.
There is also an element of vulnerability,
however; the risk that the miracle will be
relegated to that of a tall tale, a fable,
or a myth; or that it will be ridiculed,
neglected, or worse yet, treated
with indifference.

Our Heavenly Father knows us better than anyone else. There is none else save Him "that knowest (our) thoughts and the intents of (our) heart." (D&C 6:16). "O how great the holiness of our God!" cried Jacob. "For he knoweth all things, and there is not anything save he knows it." (2 Nephi 9:20). He knows when we are sleeping and He knows when we are awake. He knows when we have been good or bad, so it makes sense to do our best and to be our best, if for no other reason than to be true to the One Whose mission was to light the world.

Christmas is
the season of the year
when we remember that at one
magical moment upon a midnight
clear, there came "that glorious song
of old, from angels bending near
the earth, to touch their harps
of gold." ("It Came Upon
a Midnight Clear").

"Can there any good thing come out of Nazareth?" asked Nathanial of John, after Philip "saith unto him, We have found him, of whom Moses in the law, and the prophets, did write, Jesus of Nazareth, the son of Joseph." (John 1:45-46). And yet, it has been from Nazareth to nations far and wide, that the Gospel has spread. Religious history teaches us that it was lowly Israel, and not the mighty empires of Assyria, Babylonia, or Egypt, that became the repository of true religion. "Christianity did not go from Rome to Galilee; it was the other way around. In our day, the routing is from Palmyra to Paris, and not the reverse." (Spencer W. Kimball, C.R., 4/1978).

Christmas is the
season of the year when we
remember that "God, since the
beginning of the world, ever
sent his true prophets and
preachers of his word,
to warn the people."
(William Tyndall).

One of the greatest contributions of one of them, named Joseph Smith, was to share his knowledge of what is to come after death. He clarified our understanding of heaven and created desire in the hearts of millions to follow the path that leads Home. He promised that our wounds would be the places where light enters us, and so, we thank God for our blood, sweat, toil, and tears. (See Luke 10:34).

> Christmas is the
> season of the year when
> we appreciate that it was in
> the birth of the Savior that
> the hopes and fears of
> all the years have
> been met at
> once.

There is already enough on our plates without adding to the burden by fretting about the future. Worry is interest on a debt that may never come due. There are, after all, only three types of control in life. First, are those circumstances over which we have absolute control. Then, are those things over which we have indirect control, and finally those things over which we have no control. The gift of Christmas helps us to learn where to most profitably direct our energies and resources, and to leave to the Savior those things that we are powerless to change by ourselves.

Christmas is the season of the year when the clouds of misunderstanding evaporate before the penetrating rays of divine truth.

It is a time when His disciples are not ashamed to "declare his doing among the people." It is a time when it is easy to "make mention that his name is exalted." (2 Nephi 22:4). It is a time when those who come into the fold may more easily stand as witnesses of God. (See Mosiah 18:9).

> Christmas is
> the season of the year
> when the fire of our faith
> burns nearly as brightly as
> the Star that appeared
> over Bethlehem.

Our hearts cry out: "I love thee, Lord Jesus, look down from the sky, and stay by my cradle, till morning is nigh." ("Away in a Manger"). That dawn heralds a bright new day, full of hope and promise. It is a time for us to be about our Father's business. (See Luke 2:49). If we waste or kill that time, or even if we bide our time, we damage our eternal selves, for "in an hour when (we) think not the summer shall be past, and the harvest ended, and (our) souls not saved." (D&C 45:2).

Christmas is the season of the year when the strife of words and the contest of opinion are quieted, and in their place, all is calm and all is bright.

It was Jesus Christ who commanded the waters to be still, and they obeyed. And then, in the ensuing calm, those who were with Him "marveled, saying, What manner of man is this, that even the winds and the sea obey him!" (Matthew 8:27). Ironically, Cicero observed of the Roman Empire with a focus that was far too narrow, that "he who controls the sea, controls everything."

Christmas
is the season of
the year when we are
humbled before a Babe
lying in a manger
of straw, with
no crib for
His bed.

In the midst of our remembrance of the uncomfortable adversity and relentless opposition that were the norm for the Savior, we "submit ourselves to his nurture and chastening and (do) not withdraw ourselves from his correction." (William Tyndall, "Obedience" p. 56). We intuitively realize that, because of Him, no matter what our challenges might be, our lives are "fairy tale waiting to be written by His finger." (Hans Christian Anderson).

Christmas is
the season of the year
when we see in the Babe of
Bethlehem the acorn of a mighty
oak; One who was chosen and
foreordained from before the
foundation of the world to
grow to the full statue of
His spirit; to be our
Savior and our
Redeemer.

He was the Firstborn of the spirit children of our Heavenly Father and the greatest of all. He understood The Plan of our Father, and had already made great personal sacrifices for His pre-mortal brethren. He was "the lamb slain from the foundation of the world." (Revelation 13:8). As His Father declared: "Behold, my Beloved Son, which was my Beloved and Chosen from the beginning, (Who) said unto me – Father, Thy will be done, and the glory be Thine forever." (Moses 4:2).

Christmas is the
season of the year when
the celebration feels like a
warm coat that provides shelter
from the wind. It is when the
love light gleams, and surely,
we'll be home for Christmas,
if only in our dreams.
("I'll Be Home for
Christmas").

"I wish I could remember the days before my birth," mused the poet, "and if I knew our Father before I came to earth. In quiet moments when I'm all alone, I close my eyes and try to see my Heavenly home. Although I can't remember and cannot clearly see, I listen to the Spirit and so I must believe. But still I wonder, and I hope to find the answer to the question that is on my mind. Where is Heaven? Is it very far? I would like to know if it's beyond the brightest star." (Janice Kapp Perry). "How far is heaven? It's not very far. With people like you, it's right where you are." (Anonymous).

Christmas is
the season of
the year when our
trees are trimmed with
brightly colored lights to
remind us that our spirit "is
the candle of the Lord."
(Proverbs 20:27).

If we lose that intrinsic light as we succumb to worldly cares, we might be submitting ourselves to judgment that is nothing more than a measurement of the numbers of foot-candles remaining that we bring to the Bar of Justice. "Our birth" after all, is "a sleep and a forgetting. The soul that rises with us, our life's star, hath had elsewhere its setting, and cometh from afar. Not in entire forgetfulness, and not in utter nakedness, but trailing clouds of glory do we come, from God, who is our Home." (William Wordsworth, "Ode: Intimations of Immortality. Recollections from Early Childhood").

Christmas is the season of the year when our thoughts, that are so frequently focused on family and loved ones, turn to the friendless and the unappreciated. We might ask ourselves: If not now, when? If not me, who?

When we open our arms to those around us, we recognize that the declaration of the Savior is an affirmation, rather than an indictment: "Inasmuch as ye have done it unto the least of these, my brethren, ye have done it unto me," (Matthew 25:40). At Christmas time, and throughout the year, an ounce of our help will be far better than a pound of our preaching.

Christmas is the season of the year when our Heavenly Father sends us gifts of the Spirit. The wrapping, bows, and ribbons may change over time, but their contents remain sacred, waiting to be opened again and again, for our enjoyment and our benefit.

These will be the antidotes for a whole array of poisonous telestial tendencies that threaten to choke out the expression of celestial sureties. We recognize that we cannot be saved by simply rallying around noble principles. Instead, we will be redeemed in the precious blood of the Holy One of Israel.

Christmas is the
season of the year when
we make a quantum leap
from the world of everyday
all the way to Jesus, by giving
ourselves to Him completely
and without reservation.

"In the Last Days, our discipleship will be lived in crescendo." (Neal A. Maxwell). Those who are in step with the cadence of the Gospel understand that the blessings that follow obedience have a performance price. Hence, Brigham Young's example gives us our marching orders: "I never count the cost of anything," he declared. "I just find out what the Lord wants me to do, and I do it."

> Christmas is the season of the year when we see the fulfilment of prophesy, that "the universe can be a machine for the making of Gods."
> (Henri Bergson).

As King Benjamin declared: "Because of the covenant which you have made, you shall be called the children of Christ, his sons, and his daughters; for behold, this day he hath spiritually begotten you; for you say that your hearts are changed through faith on his name; therefore, you are born of him." (Mosiah 5:7). We believe our Redeemer, Who promised that after our sojourn in mortality, we would "shine forth as the sun in the kingdom of (our) Father." (Matthew 13:43). Finally, when our faith has been distilled into the reduction sauce of consecration, our every desire will be to glorify God until our bodies have been "filled with light," and we comprehend the solemnities of eternity. (D&C 88:67).

> Christmas is
> the season of the
> year when our secular
> education is interrupted
> by "Winter Break," allowing
> our spiritual education to
> kick into a higher gear
> during the holy days
> of our journey to
> Christ.

The graduate school of hard knocks will teach us what we learned in spiritual kindergarten. Any detours or disappointments that we experience along the way will be nothing more than bumps and potholes on the straight and narrow path leading to the Savior. It is all part of the fantastic education we receive that relates to opposition, as we travel along the highway that leads to heaven.

Christmas is
the season of the
year when the Lord's
disciples participate in
tithing settlement, when
the core temperature of
their testimony is taken
by the branch president
or the bishop who is His
representative in the
congregations of
the faithful.

Payment of a full tithe is a good barometer of spiritual maturity. Joseph Smith said that a religion that does not require the sacrifice of all things does not have the power to save our souls. It makes no difference upon which principle of the Gospel we may be focusing; the distance to the Celestial Kingdom of God is measured by active faith, and not in miles. And so, Christmas is a good time to read ourselves full, think ourselves straight, pray ourselves hot, and let ourselves go.

Christmas is the
season of the year when
we remember the circumstances
surrounding the Annunciation, and
how Mary, the mother of Jesus, had
"found favor with God." (Luke 1:30).
In that context, we remember the
Lord's repeated admonition:
"Be ye clean that bear the
vessels of the Lord."
(D&C 133:5).

"Motherhood," declared David O. McKay, "is the greatest potential influence for good in human life. The mother's image is the first that stamps itself on the unwritten page of the young child's mind. It is her caress that first awakens a sense of security; her kiss, the first realization of affection; her sympathy and tenderness, the first assurances that there is love in the world. Motherhood is the noblest calling in the world." ("Gospel Ideals," p. 452).

Christmas is
the season of the year
when we dare to consider the
possibility that we might one day
be like the Babe lying in the manger;
that we too might grow to the full
stature of our spirits, for we have
been created, as was He, in both
the image and the likeness of
God, Who is our Father.
(See Genesis 1:26).

We reflect upon the gifts of the Spirit and the power of His guidance by which we may attain His perfection and stature, so that we may enjoy not only what He has, but also what He is. If, by the grace of God, we "are perfect in Christ, and deny not His power, then are (we) sanctified in Christ by the grace of God, through the shedding of the blood of Christ ... that (we) become holy, without spot." (Moroni 10:33).

Christmas is the season of the year that finds wise men, women, and children following His Star from the four corners of the earth. They are as one body in Christ, and look to the Word of God, and live. (See Amos 5:4).

As Alma counseled his son Helaman: "It is as easy to give heed to the word of Christ," our compass, "which will point (us) to a straight course to eternal bliss, as it was for our fathers to give heed to this compass," the Liahona, "which would point unto them a straight course to the promised land. Do not let us be slothful," he urged, or move slowly, "because of the easiness of the way ... Look to God, and live." (Alma 37:37-38, & 47). Christmas is the perfect opportunity to look to God. It is up to us, whether or not we will live.

Christmas is
the season of the year
when the average American
family will complete its
annual expenditure
of $2,030.00
eating out.

On their way to restaurants, they will probably pass a homeless person or two, displaying a sign begging for food. A family of 6 will have spent nearly $5,000.00, a ward (275 active members) will have spent nearly $225,000.00, and a stake (3,000 members) will have spent nearly 2.5 million dollars. This is itself food for thought, as 820 million of God's children go to bed hungry, every night of their lives, on Christmas Eve and throughout the year.

Christmas is the
season of the year when the
bells of the Salvation Army jingle
in hopeful anticipation. Meanwhile,
pre-occupied shoppers scurry by with
sounding brass and tinkling cymbals
ringing so loudly in their ears that
they deny themselves the thrill
of being transformed into
angels who have just
received their
wings.

Without noticing, busy shoppers rush by on their way to spend $6.00 on a Starbuck's latte, or $3.50 on a plastic bottle that is likely filled with tap water. People of affluence too often "beat my people to pieces, and grind the faces of the poor, saith the Lord of Hosts." (2 Nephi 13:15). And yet, there is hope that when the bells peal "more loud and deep, they will testify that God is not dead, nor doth he sleep. The wrong shall fail, and the right prevail, with peace on earth, and good will to men." ("I Heard The Bells on Christmas Day").

Christmas is the
season of the year when
we figuratively unpackage
a stream of lights that traces the
pathway to our divine center, and we
realize that without the Redeemer
of the world to help us, they
must remain in a hopeless
tangle of confusion.

Too often, we amuse ourselves with games of Trivial Pursuit, mistaking it for the Game of Life. The real face of sin is waste. It is doing one thing, when something else of far greater good could have been done in its stead. It is settling for mediocrity when the more challenging road leads to greater heights with spectacular vistas up ahead just around the next switchback. Sin is a capitulation to spiritual stagnation and a forfeiture of eager acceptance of the excitement of eternal progression. It is trading a mess of pottage for our eternal birthright. It is nothing more than an overnight stay in a second-class hotel, when God's five star all-inclusive resort lies behind pearly gates, just down the road on the right.

> Christmas
> is the season
> of the year when we
> sit at the feet of the Lord's
> anointed and listen to their
> powerful testimonies of
> the divinity of the
> Savior of the
> world.

The very nature of their calling is to bear witness to all the world that the Babe in Bethlehem was the Son of God who taught the way to salvation and exaltation in a manner that could be easily understood. The Lord's anointed are long-suffering, unlike the money lenders of Babylon, who charge usurious interest when sharing the Good News. The Lord's anointed consecrate their resources to Him, while Babylon's land-grabbers plunder and squander the bounty that was meant to be freely shared with the world.

Christmas
is the season of the
year when we look to the
Babe in the manger, where
we hope to rediscover our
own innocence. We return
to our roots and search
for our beginnings, all
the way back to our
Heavenly Father,
Who is our
Home.

"Heaven lies about us in our infancy. Shades of the prison-house begin to close upon the growing boy; but behold, he sees the light, and whence it flows. He sees it in his joy. The youth, who daily farther from the east must travel, still is nature's priest, and by the vision splendid, is on his way attended. At length, the man perceives it die away, and fade into the light of common day." (William Wordsworth, "Ode: Intimations of Immortality").

Christmas is the season of the year when we rediscover that it was because God wanted to save us, and it was for that reason only, that He sent His Firstborn Son into the world.

He came to save those of every race, creed, color, and national origin, provided they maintain ideals and standards in harmony with those of heaven. The twinkling lights of Christmas remind us that Zion comes in many different colors. It speaks Aymara and Zulu, and dozens of other languages. It lives in nearly 3,500 stakes from Argentina to Zimbabwe. It has over 16 million members who are red, yellow, brown, black, white, and everything in between. It wears a sarong, a grass skirt, a blue collar, a tupeno, a kilt, and a business suit. It lives in igloos, huts, and high-rises. Most importantly, it shares a common testimony that Jesus is the Christ, and that His love makes the world go 'round.

> Christmas is the season of the year when the heirs of the Abrahamic Covenant proclaim that Jesus of Nazareth was born King of the Jews.

We know that one day, Israel will recognize Him as their Messiah. And so, "by the authority of the Holy Priesthood of God that has again been restored to the earth, and by the ministration under the direction of the Prophet of God, Apostles of the Lord Jesus Christ have been to the Holy Land and have dedicated that country for the return of the Jews; and we believe that in the due time of the Lord they shall be in the favor of God again. And let no Latter-day Saint be guilty of taking any part in any crusade against these people." (Heber J. Grant, C.R., 10/1921 - just two decades before the Holocaust, and 27 years before the creation of the state of Israel).

Christmas is the season of the year when, one more time, angels descend "thru cloven skies ... with peaceful wings unfurled; and still their heavenly music floats o'er all the weary world." ("It Came Upon a Midnight Clear").

For too long, the majestic clockwork and music of the holiday season has fallen on deaf ears. "Is it not a shame," asked William Tyndall in 1528, "that we Christians come so oft to church in vain, when he of four score years old knoweth no more than he that was born yesterday?" ("Obedience," p. 96-97). Christmas should be able to change the dynamics of that pessimistic equation.

Christmas is the season of the year that competes with the confusing cacophony created by telestial traffic. Yet, "ever o'er its babel sounds, the blessed angels sing." ("It Came Upon a Midnight Clear").

We "labor for knowledge, understanding, and feeling, and beware superstition and persuasion of worldly wisdom, philosophy, and of hypocrisy and ceremonies." As the Lord graciously enlightens our minds, "we walk in the plain and open truth." (William Tyndall, "Obedience" p. 78).

Christmas is the season of the year when the promise is renewed that a "new heaven and earth shall own the Prince of Peace their King; and the whole world send back the song which now the angels sing." ("It Came Upon a Midnight Clear").

Truth now blazes brightly, born of the intensity of martyr's fires. We pray that never again will the church of the devil "suffer no man to know God's word, but burn it and make heresy of it." (William Tyndall, "Obedience," p. 99).

Christmas
is the season of
the year when we see
in the gentle cough and
sweet cry of the Babe, that
God was also "present with
us in our mother's womb,
and fashioned us and
breathed life into us"
even before our
birth. (William
Tyndall).

Elohim is our Heavenly Father. His genetic code lies hidden within our DNA sequences. We were born of Him as His spirit children, acquired His qualities and characteristics, and were raised by Him to spiritual maturity, until we could progress no more as long as we remained in our first estate. So, we were added upon, leaving His presence to fulfill our mission on earth. Even now, as "strangers and pilgrims on the earth", we are yet His spirit sons and daughters who enjoy a measure of His divine nature, waiting for it to burst forth, at Christmas, in a display of celestial energy. (Hebrews 11:13).

> Christmas is
> the season of the year
> when the world may finally
> "revolve from night to day."
> ("I Heard the Bells on
> Christmas Day").

When we move from the darkness of benighted thought to the brilliant clarity of the light of truth, we will stand with Alma to "manifest unto the people that (we have) been born of God." (Alma 36:23). We will conquer the self-defeating behaviors and flawed character traits that had limited our progression. Our salvation will consist in our "being placed beyond the power of our enemies, meaning the enemies of our progression, such as dishonesty, greediness, lying, immorality, and other vices." ("Joseph Smith Diary", Willard Richards, Scribe).

Christmas is
the season of the
year when we reflect
upon the miracle that
after two millennia, the
Savior's birth remains
the Greatest Story
Ever Told.

The faithful of every age preserved and passed on the tale, although there were many for whom the Bible had become a magical book, conveying power and knowledge without the aid of revelation. Moroni envisioned those in the Last Days who had "transfigured the holy word of God," or who had changed the appearance and substance of the scriptures. (Mormon 8:33). We need the magic of Christmas to flesh out the sketchy narratives of the Gospels.

Christmas is the season of the year when the Spirit teaches us that God, Who holds the whole world in His hands, is no respecter of persons.

"He is indifferent and not partial; as great in his sight is a servant as a master." (William Tyndall, "Obedience" p. 61). There are, in fact, no ordinary people. "You have never talked to a mere mortal; it is immortals with whom we joke, work, marry, snub and exploit. Our charity must be a real and costly love; no mere tolerance or indulgence which parodies love as flippancy parodies merriment. Next to the blessed sacrament itself, your neighbor is the holiest object presented to your senses, for in him also Christ is truly hidden and glorified." (C.S. Lewis, "The Weight of Glory").

Christmas is the season of the year that encourages us "to submit ourselves and serve our brethren, and to give ourselves for them, and to win them to Christ." (William Tyndall).

"I sought to see myself. Myself I could not see. I sought to know the Lord through prayer. But He eluded me. I sought to serve my fellow men, and I found all three." (Anonymous). Sometimes, Christians wish to live within sight of a church, while others wish they could live within a hundred yards of hell. Sometimes, the Lord sends His ablest missionaries to His most wicked children. He arms them well with unwavering faith, a sure knowledge of Gospel principles, firm and abiding testimonies of the doctrines of the Kingdom, of God's Plan, and of the Savior, a blessing and setting-apart by file leaders, the continual prayers of the faithful, and an endowment of spiritual power received in holy places.

Christmas is the
season of the year when
we hear the rustling of the
robes of angels, and their voices
from the Celestial City as the sound
of trumpets speaking to us, declaring:
"Peace on earth, good will to men." And
all the while, the earth lies in solemn
stillness, unknowingly mesmerized
by the miracle of His birth.

In a literal sense, "the heavens declare the glory of God, and the firmament sheweth his handiwork. (Psalms 19:1). "His voice is heard in the rolling thunder; his speech is recorded in the lilac's bloom." (Bruce R. McConkie). The earth, the sun, the moon, and the stars "roll upon their wings in their glory, in the midst of the power of God. All these things are kingdoms, and any man who hath seen any or the least of these hath seen God moving in his majesty and power." (D&C 84:45-47).

Christmas is the season of the year when "mild He lays His glory by, born that man no more may die." ("Hark! The Herald Angels Sing"). For "this is life eternal, that they might know thee the only true God, and Jesus Christ, whom thou hast sent." (John 17:3).

Emphatically, the scriptures teach: "There is no other name given whereby salvation cometh; therefore ... take upon you the name of Christ." (Mosiah 5:8). "Yea, come unto Christ, and be perfected in him, and deny yourselves of all ungodliness; and if ye shall deny yourselves of all ungodliness, and love God with all your might, mind and strength, then is his grace sufficient for you, that by his grace ye may be perfect in Christ." (Moroni 10:32).

Christmas is the
season of the year when
we lend our voices to the angelic
host, to proclaim that Christ is born
in Bethlehem; glory to the newborn
King! "The kingdom of heaven is
at hand; yea, the Son of God
cometh in his glory, in his
might, majesty, power,
and dominion."
(Alma 5:50).

The memory of His birth could have quietly faded away, but as time passed and events unfolded, there was instead "no greater drama in human record than the sight of a few Christians, scorned or oppressed by a succession of emperors, bearing all trials with a fierce tenacity, multiplying quietly, building order while their enemies generated chaos, fighting the sword with the word, brutality with hope, and at last defeating the strongest state that history has known. Caesar and Christ had met in the arena, and Christ had won. (Will Durant, "The Story of Civilization," 3:652).

Christmas is the season of the year when we see in the Babe of Bethlehem our own passport to perfection. Christmas invites us to hitch a ride upon the coat-tails of the Gods, Who will carry us as upon the wings of eagles all the way to the portal of the Celestial Kingdom.

All who have thus been born again are set free by the perfect Law of Liberty to reach their potential. As Paul taught the Romans: "We are buried with him by baptism into death: that like as Christ was raised up from the dead by the glory of the Father, even so we also should walk in newness of life." (Romans 6:3). When we are born again, we are as the acorns of a mighty oak, vitalized by His nurturing influence to reach the full stature of our spirits.

Christmas is the
season of the year when
the universal innocence of
children creates optimism
that peace on earth may
be within our reach.

When we become as our little ones, "submissive, meek, humble, patient, (and) full of love," the enticings of the Holy Spirit will help us to put off our natural inclinations, that we might become saints through the Atonement of Jesus Christ. (Mosiah 3:19).

Christmas is the season of the year when we think less about self-sufficiency, and more about Christ dependency.

We realize that His message was intended to change our nature, that we might progress to the point where we reflect His attributes in perfection. Our chaste behavior reveals our love of all of our Heavenly Father's children. Our righteous stewardship is a shadow of His omnipotence. As the Spirit expands the boundaries of our faith, we quietly scratch the surface of our comprehension of omniscience. We begin to appreciate the meaning of Christmas, and we inaugurate our own journey to Bethlehem, Gethsemane, Calvary, the Garden Tomb, and the Silver City.

Christmas
is the season of the
year when our wallets
are empty, but more
importantly, our
hearts are
full.

The lines between "want" and "need" are often blurred by those who focus on telestial trinkets and temporal trash. Such individuals have difficulty recognizing the differences between poverty and wealth. We are more comfortably in our natural element when we yearn for spiritual gifts rather than the profane baubles and ornaments of the world.

Christmas is the
season of the year when many
give only lip service to the story
of the Christ Child. They may draw
near unto Him with their mouths, but
their hearts are far from Him, and
their fear of the Lord is faulty,
inasmuch as it is based upon
the precepts of men.
(See 2 Nephi 27:25).

Each year as we open our scriptures to the Book of Luke, we would do well to remember the caution penned by Sir Walter Scott as a self-reminder on the flyleaf of his personal Bible: "Within this awful volume lies the mystery of mysteries. Happiest is he of human race, to whom our God has given grace, to read, to fear, to hope, to pray; to lift the latch, and force the way. And better had he ne'er been born, who reads to doubt, or reads to scorn."

Christmas is the season of the year when our hope in Christ assures us of inner peace, that our lives are headed in the right direction, and that the Lord loves us.

"Be still, and know that I am God," He said. (D&C 101:16). With that quiet confirmation, comes the admonition to see that we serve Him with all our heart, might, mind and strength. (D&C 4:2). All that He asks of us is that we focus our affections, will-power, reasoning faculties, and physical efforts on our worship of Him and His beloved Son. To help us to do that, He gave us not only the Greatest Story Ever Told, to read at Christmas time and throughout the year, but also the Holy Ghost to bear witness of its veracity. (See John 14:6).

Christmas
is the season of
the year that gives
us the opportunity to
recognize that each of us
lives on a kind of spiritual
credit, and that one day, our
account will be closed
and a settlement will
be required.

"My father focuses heart-gripping flashes across the wall screen. Family slides. I am small, my brother is smaller, and my sister is smallest. Days now dead re-open like old storybooks from memory's heaped box. Soberly, I think of another Father, Who someday shall open my mind, and flash reeling remembering of every day's minute across my soul, across the heavens, and kindly ask me to narrate." (Lora Lyn Stucker, "New Era," 8/1973).

Christmas is the season of the year when headlines shout out the encouraging news that consumers, recovering from their Thanksgiving feasts, have parted with billions of dollars in a single, frenzied, Black Friday shopping spree. We only pray that their hard-earned money has been well spent.

Items that are "on sale" encourage us to spend so that we can save money. Retailers pray to gods of wood and stone for a lucrative Chritma $eason. Are we all mad? A judge asked the jury: "Have you reached a verdict?" "We have, Your Honor," responded the foreman. "We find the defendant not guilty, by reason of insanity." To which the Judge exclaimed: "What? All twelve of you?" We go collectively crazy during the Christmas season, trying to outspend each other in a tangible demonstration of our misguided generosity. The spirit of Christmas is the only thing that can help to dig us out of the hole we have created for ourselves by thinking that by exporting our wealth we can win friends and influence people, and that money can buy happiness.

Christmas is the season of the year when we may awaken to a fresh blanket of snow covering the land. We are reminded of the words of Isaiah, who said: "Though your sins be as scarlet, they shall be as white as snow." (Isaiah 1:18).

"Many people seem to have the idea that the Judgment will somehow involve weighing or balancing, with their good deeds on one side of the scales and their bad deeds on the other. This notion is false. God cannot allow moral or ethical imperfection in any degree whatsoever to dwell in his presence. He cannot tolerate sin with the least degree of allowance." (Steven Robinson, "What The Mormons Believe"). This is why God sent the Savoir into the world, and why His Atonement is infinite in its scope; He has the power to literally redeem us from every sin we have ever committed; to be as pure as freshly-fallen snow.

> Christmas
> is the season of
> the year when we see
> that it is because of its
> unyielding standard in the
> face of the homogenizing
> influence of the world,
> that the Gospel is the
> "Good New" to those
> who embrace
> it.

It provides all the principles, doctrines, ordinances, and covenants that enable us to become sanctified so that we may be worthy to live once again in a state of holiness in the presence of our Heavenly Father. Because of the Gospel, we may all come unto Christ, "lay hold upon every good gift ... and be perfected in him." (Moroni 10:32). If we "continue in the supplicating of his grace," we will stand blameless before Him at His Pleasing Bar. (Alma 7:3).

Christmas is the season of the year when New Year's Resolutions cannot be far away.

For many, the emphasis just after the holidays is on intangible resolutions - promises that we make to ourselves that generally are kept for a few days or weeks at best, before they are abandoned, and we return to our previously held lifestyle. We should take a lesson from the Apostles, whose ministry was documented by Acts, and not by resolutions.

Christmas
is the season of
the year when we look
forward to a wonderful
dinner, complete with a
turkey or goose, and
all the trimmings.

We soberly think of another gathering, even the Banquet of Consequences, where there will not be much at the table that is satisfying, unless we are able to bow our heads in reverence, and not hang them in shame, in the presence of Christ, Who will be there, to serve us our just desserts. (See Marion D. Hanks, BYU Speeches of The Year, 10/3/1967). As we contemplate the nourishing food that is before us, we remember the words of Nephi, who said that we should "press forward, feasting upon the word of Christ." (2 Nephi 31:20).

Christmas
is the season of the
year when we hang our
stockings by the chimney with
care, in the mistaken belief
that it is Saint Nick, and
not the Savior, who is
coming to town.

As we dump out their contents on Christmas morning and a cornucopia of treats cascades onto the floor, it strikes us that our Father in Heaven has promised to open for us "the windows of heaven, and pour out a blessing that there shall not be room enough to receive it." (2 Nephi 24:10). That blessing began with His greatest Gift of all on that first Christmas morning, and it has continued every waking moment thereafter, for all His sons and daughters.

> Christmas is
> the season of the
> year when we engage
> in random acts of kindness
> that have received the divine
> approbation of our Father in
> Heaven; that are shining
> examples of quiet
> Christianity in
> action.

We need inspiration to lead us to those in need, and so we are doubly blessed as we simultaneously give even as we receive. But "looking for the spectacular, we often miss the constant flow of revealed communication that comes." (Spencer W. Kimball, "Church News," 1/5/1974). In contrast to the marketing messages of Madison Avenue that are pleasing to those with itching ears and carnal natures, the whisperings of the Spirit at Christmas time strike our more sensitive and selective chords.

Christmas is the season of the year that provides us with a wonderful opportunity to take a few halting steps on our journey to Christ; to kneel in reverent adoration before His manger with the shepherds who only moments before had been quietly tending their flocks by night.

Our own journey begins in Bethlehem, and then moves on to Galilee and His Judean ministry. It winds its way through Jerusalem, Gethsemane, and Calvary, and finally to an empty tomb outside the city walls. As we walk with the Savior, we try to remain anxiously engaged in good causes, do many things of our own free will, and bring to pass much righteousness, for we realize the power has always been within us, wherein we are agents unto ourselves. (See D&C 58:27-28).

> Christmas
> is the season of the
> year when the eyes of
> our understanding are
> opened, and eternal
> possibilities are
> unfolded to
> our view.

At Christmas, our souls venture forth from their normal dwelling places "and, discarding the poor lenses of the body, peer thru the telescope of truth into the infinite reaches of immortality." (Helen Keller, "My Religion," p. 76). The Babe in the manger helps us to avert the one tragedy in life worse than to be born without sight, and that is to be born with sight, but without vision.

> Christmas
> is the season of
> the year that reminds
> us that it is because of
> the Savior's restoration
> of truth and of light
> that our age need
> be retrospective
> no longer.

Third-person accounts of the Lord's birth and ministry are insufficient. Religious foundations are not based on historical events; they rest upon the footings of revelation. When we hunger and thirst after righteousness, we partake of the Bread of Life and draw from a fountain of living waters. The story of the birth of the Savior becomes our personal possession; it is incorporated into the fabric of our being. Christmas joy is meant to be shared, for it belongs to the world.

> Christmas is
> the season of the
> year when His disciples
> acknowledge the good
> in all of God's children,
> whether they be wealthy
> or poor, ignorant or
> wise, or learned
> or untaught.

Christianity has become the most extensive and universal religion in history and claims as adherents a majority of the population in two thirds of the world's 238 countries. 1.9 billion people, 31% of the world's population, are members of over 33,000 identifiable denominations. Islam follows with 1.2 billion people. There are 14 million Jews. (Source: "World Christian Encyclopedia"). The message of the missionaries of The Church of Jesus Christ of Latter-day Saints is not intended to diminish in any way the witness of Christ of any of these people of good will. The purpose of their ministry is "that faith might increase in the earth." (D&C 1:21). Their efforts are oriented toward lighting the world with testimony that Jesus is the Christ, the Son of the Living God.

> Christmas is the season of the year when we draw upon the lessons of religious history to give us vitally needed perspective.

We ought not measure the quality of our experiences by the hopes and enjoyments of this world, but by the preparations we make for another journey, looking forward to what we shall become, rather than backward to what we have been. If we incorporate into our lives the vision of our Heavenly Father, we will see that the past is prologue, in the sense that it is an introduction to the great adventure upon which we will embark if we follow through on His Plan. What has come before doesn't matter in the grand scheme of things, because a new future lies before us, subject to the choices we make. The past may define the present, but it does not determine our future. Heavenly Father has promised us the companionship of the Holy Ghost to shepherd us through our experiences toward the Light in the East, which is where our eternal destiny lies. That is why we celebrate Christmas.

Christmas is the season of the year when we turn to God's own journal narrative to read for ourselves the circumstances surrounding the birth of His Son.

"I shall speak unto the Jews and they shall write it; and I shall also speak unto the Nephites and they shall write it; and I shall also speak unto the other tribes of the house of Israel, which I have led away, and they shall write it; and I shall also speak unto all nations of the earth and they shall write it." (2 Nephi 29:12).

> Christmas is
> the season of the year
> when we can turn to music
> and the spoken word to hear
> prophets of God bless the
> world with inspired
> testimony.

Joseph Smith and his successor prophets have all testified as Special Witnesses of the saving principles and ordinances of the Gospel of Jesus Christ. They are Prophets when they teach the body of known truth, Seers when they see with spiritual eyes and teach hidden truth, and Revelators each time they bring to the attention of the world truth that has never before been revealed. Their words are music to our ears. They touch the mystic chords of memory to create a melody that reminds us of our former Home.

> Christmas
> is the season of
> the year when, with the
> nearly universal celebration
> of the birth of our Savior Jesus
> Christ, all of God's children are
> blessed with the opportunity
> to "fear the Lord and to
> stand in awe of him."
> (Psalms 33:8).

With our free will, two conditions become immediately obvious: the opportunity to make choices in an atmosphere of opposition, and the necessity of facing the consequences that are associated with those choices. The urgency of reconciliation to the laws of heaven through atonement is not so apparent, but it is even more important. Through His prophet, the Lord has warned: "I have spoken it, I will also bring it to pass; I have purposed it, I will also do it. Hearken unto me, ye stouthearted, that are far from righteousness." (Isaiah 46:10-11). At Christmas time, we fear the Lord, but in a good way if we use our agency correctly, and we stand in awe.

*Christmas
is the season of the year
when the Word is revealed once
again to all of God's children; to
those who are both literate and
untutored in the grammar
of the Gospel.*

Christmas is a primer to bring us unto Christ. Continual guidance from the Spirit, known as revelation, is critical to vital religion, for it "cannot be maintained and preserved on the theory that God dealt with our human race only in the far past ages, and that the Bible is the only evidence we have that our God is a living, revealing, communicating God. If God ever spoke, He is still speaking. He is the great I Am, not the great He was." (Rufus Jones, "Time" Magazine, 10/11/1948).

Christmas is the season
of the year that implores us
to try even harder to overcome
evil with goodness. With tenderness
and benevolence, and with forbearance,
we attempt to turn stony hearts to the
Source of their being, even as God
with softness and kindness, and
with patience, won our hearts
with nothing more than
a little Child.

As we struggle in our efforts to stem the advancing tide of evil, we remember that it is better to light a candle than to curse the darkness. A thousand points of light, taken together, cast a very long shadow. The sage observation has never been more timely: "To sin by silence, when words should be spoken, makes cowards of men." The Savior gives us courage to follow up our thoughts and our words with deeds, for as James taught: "Faith without works is dead, being alone." (James 2:17).

Christmas is the
season of the year when we see
that "repentance goeth before faith,
and prepareth the way to Christ and
to the promises. For Christ cometh
not but to them that see their
sins in the law, and repent."
(William Tyndall).

The great blessing of repentance is that by allowing us to become clean in the sight of God, we get moving again on the pathway to perfection. After repentance, God will remember our sins no more. It is true that we might recall them, insofar as they increase our testimonies and make us more stalwart soldiers in the Army of Christ. But we will no longer be worn down by guilt or be estranged from the Spirit. We will be released from bondage to sin, which is the most liberating gift of Christmas.

Christmas is
the season of the year
when "sweet are these strains
of redeeming love," sent as a
"message of mercy from heaven
above." ("Far, Far Away on
Judea's Plains").

Our hope of mercy leads us to repentance and forgiveness because of the Atonement of Christ. The miracle of our transformation is that we develop the very nature and character of the Savior. We experience the reality of His explicit promise: "All that I have, I could give to you, but what I am, you must earn for yourself, line upon line, and precept upon precept." (See Isaiah 28:10).

Christmas is the season of the year when we look up into the heavens, and try to imagine the awe of those who witnessed how "it came to pass that a new star did appear." (3 Nephi 1:21).

In the process, the Saints in the New World became additional witnesses to the birth of the Savior. As a result, they began "to have peace in the land. And there were no contentions." (3 Nephi 1:23-24). The Star in the East was symbolic of their focus on Jesus Christ and the miracle that had come to pass in far-away Bethlehem. His Gospel became their fortification, and obedience to covenants their sanctuary against the winds of wickedness that were stirring in the land.

> Christmas is the season of the year when we "hail the Son of Righteousness", our imperfections notwithstanding. ("Hark The Herald Angels Sing").

Against the backdrop of His marvelous light, our sins bring us sorrow. We feel terrible about them. We feel profoundly filthy. We want to unload and abandon them. We are almost obsessive-compulsive about cleansing our souls. We are broken in heart, and are contrite, but we realize that in and of ourselves we are powerless to change. So, we are prepared to receive the things of the Spirit; we are teachable. With this level of commitment, we are prepared to ask, as did those on the Day of Pentecost: "What shall we do?" The straightforward answer is: "Repent and be baptized every one of you in the name of Jesus Christ for the remission of sins." (Acts 2:37-38). Only then, will there be peace on earth, and good will toward men.

Christmas is the season of the year when "love's pure light ... with the dawn of redeeming grace" streams from the face of the Babe of Bethlehem. ("Silent Night").

Without that light, we risk being seduced by a siren song that can create an insatiable desire for the world's goods. With blurred vision, we may trade life on the straight and narrow path for what we think is a much-needed vacation in Idumea. If we follow through on that misguided temptation, and check ourselves in to "Fantasy Island", we will lose power, purpose, and focus. If we think that it is better to rely more on our own strength than upon spiritual preparedness, we will be more inclined in times of crisis to grasp at the world's goods, rather than to drop to our knees, hold tightly to our faith, and with the help of our Father in Heaven, dig our way out of our problems.

Christmas is
the season of the
year that invites us to
do more than simply multiply
mirrors or study angles. If we
pay attention to principles, our
Heavenly Father will invite the
Holy Ghost to illuminate the
way before us by permitting
us to see with the eyes of
our understanding the
heavenly light that
envelops His
Son.

The Church of Jesus Christ of Latter-day Saints stands as another witness of Jesus Christ and of the Restoration of His Gospel in the Last Days. Before we united ourselves with the Saints, we stood on neutral ground. Having entered into the fold through the strait and narrow way of baptism, however, we can never again have it both ways. Those who have seen the Light become His ambassadors, willing to stand as His witnesses "at all times and in all places", but especially during the Christmas season. (Mosiah 18:9).

Christmas is the season of the year when all of us raise our eyes beyond the limited horizon of our sight. We stare in wonder at the light that is gathering in the East.

With the Wise Men of old, we ask "Where is he that is born King of the Jews? For we have seen his star ... and are come to worship him." (Matthew 2:2). With an awakening understanding, it strikes us that the new Star in the East is the Light of the World, beckoning us to follow His Shining Example.

> Christmas is the
> season of the year
> when we try to be as
> the Good Samaritan; to
> remember that an ounce
> of help is almost always
> better than a pound
> of preaching.

"We have paused on some plateaus long enough. Let us resume our journey forward and upward. Let us quietly put an end to our reluctance to reach out to others, whether in our own families, wards, or neighborhoods. We have been diverted at times from fundamentals upon which we must now focus, in order to move forward as a person or as a people." (Spencer W. Kimball, C.R., 4/1979). As Gordon B. Hinckley re-affirmed: "The Church cannot hope to save us on Sunday, if during the week it is a complacent witness to the destruction of our soul." ("Helping Others to Help Themselves," Church Welfare Pamphlet, 1945).

Christmas
is the season of
the year when the Holy
Ghost answers questions
we never thought to ask,
with spiritual statements
that are undeniable
and irrefutable.

The Spirit will illuminate our minds with answers, but only after we have posed good questions. When the Psalmist wrote: "Be still, and know that I am God," he knew that in quiet moments at Christmas time, we would experience spiritual symmetry and balance that would allow us to enjoy a profound comprehension in response to our petitions. (Psalms 46:10).

> Christmas is the
> season of the year when our
> shopping lists grow longer and
> longer, while the Savior's spiritual
> to-do list remains surprisingly
> short, to wit: "If ye love me,
> keep my commandments."
> (John 14:15).

And so, it is a good time of the year to remember Gordon B. Hinckley's Christmas Wish List: "Be grateful, be smart, be involved, be clean, be true, be positive, be humble, be still, and be prayerful." ("Way to Be: Nine Rules For Living The Good Life"). All we can hope for is to be taught what is best for ourselves and for the Kingdom of God, to develop a testimony that it should be, and then to work with all our capacity to make it happen, whatever the cost. Then, when we are richly blessed far beyond the measure that we deserve, the price, so painfully paid, will be recalled in gladness, and we will receive full value.

> Christmas is the season of the year when we are less concerned with telestial trinkets and more focused on celestial sureties.

During the Christmas season, it is very difficult to tell just what will bring us happiness. All around us in the world, we can see that both poverty and wealth have failed miserably. Neither fame nor anonymity seems to hold the key. It appears that neither sickness nor health has the ability. Both principalities and the absence of worldly influence are woefully inadequate. By all appearances, neither beauty nor the beast has the advantage. Let us not forget that there are both dark threads and "threads of gold and silver, in the pattern God has planned." (Benjamin Malachi Franklin).

Christmas
is the season of the
year when all the world is
invited to both publicly and
privately thank our Father in
Heaven for the gift of our Lord
and Savior Jesus Christ, Who was
willing to assume our debt to
Justice, to pay for our sins,
and to negotiate through
Mercy the pointed and
specific terms of our
redemption.

It is by the grace of God that we may become perfect in Christ. If we do not deny His power, the time will come when we will be "sanctified in Christ by the grace of God, through the shedding of the blood of Christ, which is in the covenant of the Father unto the remission of our sins, that we become holy, without spot." (Moroni 10:33). This is the essence of the many gifts we receive at the hands of the Christ Child.

Christmas is the season of the year when we warm ourselves before the fire of the love and friendship that we share with others.

It is a time when salutations of "Merry Christmas" and "Happy Holidays" come from our hearts as well as from our lips, and our eggnog toasts reflect our yearning that "the Lord may bless and keep us; that His countenance may shine upon us, and bring us peace; that our hearts may be full, our lives long, and our days as sweet as an Irish song." (See Psalms 67:1).

Christmas
is the season of
the year when, if we
listen very carefully,
we can hear the
gentle rustling
of angels'
wings.

"Through cloven skies they come with peaceful wings unfurled, and still their heavenly music floats o'er all the weary world." ("It Came Upon a Midnight Clear"). At Christmas time, when our minds and our spirits are unhurried, and we shake ourselves free from temporal cares and trivial concerns, the reality of the eternities can be illuminating as enlightenment opens up undreamed of vistas of otherwise inaccessible experience.

> Christmas is
> the season of the
> year when someone
> on a sidewalk is
> always ringing
> a bell.

From the Christmas-time motion picture classic "It's a Wonderful Life," we recall the angel Clarence, who finally earned his wings. Our hearts are warmed as we remember that it was the tinkling of bells that marked the occasion. It really does no violence to our faith to dream that we can soar, as do the angels. After all, Peter Pan told Wendy: "Come with me, where dreams are born. Just think of happy things, and your heart will fly on wings, forever, in Never Land!" As he further explained: "To have faith is to have wings." Who knows? Perhaps the angels who come to carry us Home will wrap us in their wings and lift us heavenward, as we take the second star on the right, and fly straight on 'til morning.

> Christmas is the season of the year when we can renew our acquaintance with the scriptures, in particular, those that speak of our Savior's birth.

It is a time to ponder and pray and move deliberately, rather than wander and play, and swing about uncontrollably on the monkey jungle of life. At Christmas time, our scripture study is not a race. We can spend time focusing on the events surrounding the birth of the Savior, turning them over and over in our minds. To develop fresh perspectives as the Spirit touches the eyes of our understanding, we need only read ourselves full, think ourselves straight, pray ourselves hot, and let ourselves go.

Christmas
is the season
of the year when we find
ourselves on a hiatus from our
academic pursuits. If we allow
the Holy Ghost to influence
us, He will provide divine
tutorial training, that we
might receive the gift
of wisdom that no
textbook can
provide.

As the Spirit enlarges our understanding, the word of God will bloom with hidden meanings we hadn't been aware of, and their applications will later pop into our minds at just the right moments. In a wonderfully whole and complete way, God will be sensitive to our needs. He will teach us how to reach out and touch the swaddling clothes of the Babe of Bethlehem, and to draw upon His virtue when our own reserves are dangerously low. (See Mark 5:27-34).

> Christmas
> is the season
> of the year that has
> the power to transform
> our obedience from a
> minor inconvenience
> into our quest.

It is one of the hardest things for the unconverted to understand that when we are diligent in our obedience, our free will enjoys its greatest expression. Unprincipled character is easily swayed by the siren song so seductively sent by Satan, and undisciplined minds crumble in the face of telestial temptations that are so tantalizing and yet so traumatizing. The less we focus on the idols of the day, the more we will recognize the legitimate rule of heaven that governs our affairs.

Christmas
is the season of the year
when The Greatest Story Ever Told is
recounted yet again, when we are invited by
the Holy Ghost to walk "where Jesus walked in
days of long ago; to wander down each path He
knew, with reverent steps and slow. Those little
lanes, they have not changed; a sweet peace
fills the air. Today I walked where Jesus
walked," and felt His comfort there.
("Today I Walked Where
Jesus Walked").

"Not enjoyment, and not sorrow is our destined end or way; but to act, that each tomorrow might find us farther than today. Lives of great men and women all remind us that we can make our lives sublime, and departing, leave behind us footprints on the sands of time. Let us then be up and doing, with a heart for any fate; still achieving, still pursuing. Learn to labor, and to wait." (Henry Wadsworth Longfellow, "A Psalm of Life").

Christmas is
the season of the year
that finds us one holiday
closer to our Home. It will be
a joyous reunion, but for now
we need to make the most of
whatever time we have left,
because it's our turn on
earth. They say that the
last six months of
our mission will
be the best, so
Carpe Diem!

"Here you are, home from your mission. Think of the people you met, the people you helped, and how you have grown, physically and spiritually. There is mother, waiting to embrace you, and standing just a bit behind father, who is bursting with pride. Are those tears of happiness on her cheeks? Father first strikes hands with you, then embraces you warmly. You are shown to your room; it is ready for your homecoming. The feelings are resonant, and you know this is where you belong, home with Heavenly Father and Mother." (Anonymous).

Christmas is
the season of the year
when, all around us, we see
mere mortals dressed as elves
and Santa Claus, reindeer with
red noses, striped candy canes,
and even an occasional green
eyed grinch. Without intending
to decorate a lump of coal in
giftwrap, it could be said that
all of these are the creations
of a diluted doctrine that
does not have the power
to transform lives. It's
all sizzle without
the steak.

Insult is added to injury when hypocrisy is accompanied by humanized and spiritually impotent creeds, when people do not really believe, but are only professors of a holy day that has become a caricature of God's design. When dogma perverts the right way of the Lord, it is an abomination in His sight. Form without substance requires that we base our faith on corrupted principles that wil not provide needed support when we greet the dawn on Christmas morning.

Christmas is the season of the year when we are invited by the Spirit to commit to our Savior all our heart, might, mind, and strength; to take up our cross and follow Him.

Jacob used the term "Saints" to describe those who believe in the Holy One of Israel. (2 Nephi 9:18). They have endured the crosses of the world, and deny themselves "all ungodliness, and every worldly lust, and keep (the) commandments." (J.S.T. Matthew 16:25-26).

Christmas
is the season
of the year when
our own experiences
are subtly interwoven
into the tapestry of
the Gospels that
testify of the
ministry of
Christ.

That coat of many colors takes the form of a recognizable and spiritually coherent pattern of stability and power that can change our lives. When we clothe ourselves in such vestments, we experience a spiritual rebirth, not only of maturation, but also of generation.

> Christmas is the season
> of the year when God gives
> us the opportunity to gauge our
> response to the birth of His Son, as
> well as to rehearse how we will
> really feel at His Second
> Coming.

How we engage Christmas is a dry run, as it were. It is a window on our world that provides insight into how we will accept the Savior at His Second Coming. Our celebration of Christmas helps us to avoid the conundrum of those who will ask at that time: "What are these wounds in Thine hands?" (D&C 45:51).

Christmas is the season of the year that hits very close to home, when we realize that it is we of whom the poets have spoken; that the Lord was "born to raise the sons and daughters of earth; born to give them second birth." ("Hark! The Herald Angels Sing").

"God hath promised Christ's merits unto all, so that whosoever repenteth is immediately beloved of Him." (William Tyndall). That same spirit came upon the people of Zarahemla, who "were filled with joy, having received a remission of their sins, and having peace of conscience, because of the exceeding faith which they had in Jesus Christ." (Mosiah 4:3).

> Christmas
> is the season
> of the year when
> "with wondering awe,
> the Wise Men saw the star
> in heaven springing, and with
> delight, in peaceful night, they
> heard the angels singing."
> ("With Wondering Awe").

When the new star appeared above Bethlehem, the kings of the East, the mighty and the high-born, came to Jerusalem, and then to Bethlehem, as witnesses of the heavenly choir and the Babe in the manger. But they took no honor unto themselves, and after leaving their gifts of gold, frankincense, and myrrh with the Christ Child, they quietly left Judea by another way. Contrast their humility with that of the supposed Vicar of Christ, who, William Tyndall reported, commanded the angels themselves to release souls from Purgatory. "Howbeit," Tyndall dryly remarked: "I am not yet certified whether they obeyed or not." ("Obedience," p. 123).

Christmas is the season of the year when there "still is found, the world around, the old and hallowed story." ("With Wondering Awe").

The Greatest Story Ever Told will forever be passed on by the authorized and inspired servants of the Lord, called to preach faith and repentance to every nation, kindred, tongue, and people. Faith will increase in the world "by hearing those who are sent from God and preacheth His promises." (William Tyndall, "Obedience," p. 122).

Christmas is the season of the year when "angels we have heard on high," are "sweetly singing o'er the plain." ("Angels We Have Heard on High").

The shepherds were the first to hear the music and see the angels, and their lesson is that the poor, the unlearned, the common person, and the native born, may come unto Christ. In these and other passages, the scriptures teach about the universality of God's love for His children, all of whom desperately need the gift of a Redeemer.

Christmas is the season of the year when "good tidings are sounding to us and each nation, and shortly the hour of redemption will come." ("Now Let us Rejoice").

The Savior said that we must be perfect in order to inherit the kingdom of God. Perhaps He meant that we should be perfect in our repentance. After explaining to his people the great Plan of Redemption that solved the dilemma created by God's demand for perfection coupled with our inability to live sinless lives, the prophet Jacob simply stated: "O be wise; what can I say more?" Quid magis possum dicire? Moroni echoed his message: "Be wise in the days of your probation: strip yourselves of all uncleanness ... Ask with a firmness unshaken, that ye will yield to no temptation, but that ye will serve the true and living God." (Mormon 9:28).

Christmas is the season of the year when "joyful all (the) nations rise (and) join the triumph of the skies." ("Hark! The Herald Angels Sing").

We are heirs of God and joint-heirs with Christ when we follow the covenant path. (See Romans 8:17). It is then that the bands of death will be broken, and we will be set free by His grace. There is no other name given whereby salvation cometh," said Benjamin; "therefore, I would that ye should take upon you the name of Christ, all you that have entered into the covenant with God." (Mosiah 5:8).

Christmas is
the season of the year
when we pray with the angels
in heaven: "Hasten the time when,
from every clime, men shall unite in
the strains sublime. Glory to God in the
highest. Peace on earth, good will to men."
("Far, Far Away on Judea's Plains").

We pray for a unity of the faith during the Christmas season, when we "talk of Christ, rejoice in Christ, preach of Christ, prophesy of Christ, and write according to our prophecies, that our children may know to what source they may look for a remission of their sins." (2 Nephi 25:26).

Christmas
is the season
of the year when His
disciples determine to help
their less fortunate brethren
"to bear their weakness, (to be)
courteous unto them, to win them
unto Christ, and to overcome them
with kindness." (William Tyndall).

His disciples are always ready to give courage and hope, and to speak kind words that awaken to cheerfulness the souls of others, 'til heart meets with heart "and rejoices in friendship that ever is true." ("Let Us Oft Speak Kind Words"). Their charity is founded upon forgiveness, triggered by tolerance, affected by appreciation, and reflected in respect. Their kind words are as keys that unlock the gates of heaven.

> Christmas is
> the season of the
> year when the Savior
> of the world is revealed
> yet again, with another
> encore performance
> on the center
> stage of
> life.

The panorama unfolds before our eyes. Gift-giving may put us in the mood, carols may arouse us, and Nativity Scenes may stir us, but we receive His sure witness in dreams and visions, by voices, promptings, a burning in the bosom, and in strokes of inspiration on Christmas Eve. "For God speaketh once, yea twice, yet (we) perceiveth it not. In a dream, in a vision of the night, when deep sleep falleth upon (us), in slumberings upon the bed; then he openeth (our) ears ... and sealeth (our) instruction." (Job 33:14-16).

Christmas is the season of the year when the faith of the children of God is to believe what they have not seen with their natural eyes. But the reward of their faith will be when God opens the eyes of their understanding, that they might see what they believe.

As faith intensifies, the Lord's glory will rest upon His people. The meaning of Christmas will be revealed in marvelous simplicity and plainness. The servants of Jesus Christ will enjoy an endowment of power as angels watch over them, guiding them, directing them, and protecting them. His kingdom will roll forth even as the walls of Babylon crumble and fall. Oases will spring up in the desert and living water will slake the thirst of a people eager for something in which they may trust, in which they may place their faith, and in which they may believe with all their hearts and souls.

> Christmas is the season of the year that encourages us to perform an annual self-diagnostic evaluation.

We re-examine our priorities, enlarge our perceptions to unleash a larger view of life, release the Spirit to unlock our potential, and yield our will to His in order to tap into His power. If we surrender our dreams to the narrow and confining reality of the carnal and sensual world, we will suffer a defeat of cosmic proportion. However, when our behavior is in harmony with Gospel principles, we will find ourselves in a constant state of improvement leading to perfection. In the process, we will be empowered to become what we had heretofore scarcely dreamed possible. Christmas is the foundation stone of the Gospel, which is the perfect law of liberty, and its gift of truth will set us free. (See John 8:32).

> Christmas is
> the season of the year
> when, too often, we "strangle
> ourselves with what we can buy,
> things whose opacity further
> obstructs our ability to see
> what is already there."
> (Gretel Erlich).

One of the greatest challenges faced by our society is its insatiable desire for immediate gratification. We are frustrated by the limitations of our RAM and our cell phones, and the slow speed of our micro-processors. The violation of the 10th commandment is a cholesterol that can clog spiritual arteries. Our society is blinded to its sobering similarity to an addict's progressive tolerance and destructive reliance upon the chemo-therapeutic equivalents of gods of wood and stone. Christmas invites us all to enroll in Heavenly Father's rehab program. Its centerpiece relies on a spiritual angioplasty designed to rebuild damaged faith, heal broken hearts, restore shattered dreams, and loose the shackles of every form of bondage.

Christmas is the season of the year when we are overcome by an enthusiasm that is simply the divine fire of God.

"For unto us a child is born; unto us a son is given." (Isaiah 9:6) In the initial stages of our spiritual awakening, our testimony of the Mighty God, the Everlasting Father, and the Prince of Peace is born in the classical sense, with physical and emotional struggle. It is born of foundation faith in the Babe of Bethlehem and in the principles of His Gospel. Then, we bear our testimonies by carrying them to others, because we are perpetually thrilled with life, are possessed by the Spirit, and enjoy celestial inspiration.

Christmas is the season of the year when we see our own renewal reflected in the Newborn Babe in the manger.

When our lives conform to the pattern established by the Christ Child, and the eyes of our spiritual understanding are opened, scales of darkness will fall away and the Savior will become our hope. (See Jeremiah 14:8). If our letters to Santa are redirected to Him after being edited for content, and our Christmas wishes are without guile, He will make it possible for us to become the happiest people among all those who have ever been created by the hand of God. (See 4 Nephi 1:15-17).

> Christmas is the season of the year when we view the circumstances that surrounded the Savior's birth against a wealth of doctrine imbedded in a historical matrix that touches on reality in a thousand different ways.

In the first century BCE, Cicero wrote: "The first law for the historian is that he shall never dare utter an untruth. The second is that he shall suppress nothing that is true. Moreover, there shall be no suspicion of partiality or of malice in his writing." Luke's account of the birth of the Savior was true to this mandate. It "illuminates reality, vitalizes memory, provides guidance in daily life, and brings us tidings of antiquity." It is the "evidence of time, the light of truth, the life of memory, and the directress of life, committed to immortality." (Cicero, "De Oratore," ii, 36). In its passages, "the centuries roll back to the ancient age of gold." (Horace, "Odes," IV, ii, 39).

> Christmas is the season of the year when the Law of Witnesses enjoys its most profound fulfillment.

The witnesses of the birth of Christ invite us to recognize and accept the truth. The Star above Bethlehem shines down upon both shepherds in the fields and Wise Men who have come from out of the world to adore Him. A heavenly host of angels hovers just beyond a parted veil to confirm the reality of the Greatest Story Ever Told. Their depositions speak to us from the dust of time, and we devour them as we would the Bread of Life. Every Christmas we feast upon His Word as we seek, yearn, strive, and wrestle for our own blessing.

Christmas is the season of the year when a drama of all encompassing proportion is once again revealed to the world.

The Savior is the Star of David. His name appears in blazing light on a heavenly marquee above Bethlehem. Our witness is accompanied by the rising tenor of a celestial symphony that has been scored for every imaginable instrument. The orchestration of Christmas prepares us for our Senior Recital that will showcase our command of the pitch, rhythm, dynamics, timbre, and texture of the Gospel. Along the way, Christmases past and present guide us back to the Source of our inspiration. We visualize ourselves at His manger, kneeling at the feet of the Maestro. There, we will enjoy master classes from Him Who first created musicality by matching movement and form to the melody and mood of His celestial creation on that first Christmas morning.

Christmas is the season of the year when we remember the irritation in the voice of the innkeeper, who impatiently barked out that there was no room at the inn.

We contrast his behavior with the repetitive teaching moments in the home of Joseph and Mary, where charity must have been practiced as well as preached. It was they who reacquainted the Son of God with the perfect fit of His personalized divine design. The first Christmas, and thirty Christmases thereafter, prepared Him to complete His dissertation on life. Two thousand years after the successful defense of His thesis, it is still recognized as the world's magnum opus.

> Christmas is the
> season of the year
> when too many confuse
> selfish indulgence with
> the merriment of
> the holidays.

Intemperance and drunkenness impair the judgment of the weak-willed, who are held captive because their crippled character can no longer receive insight, intuition, discernment, inspiration, or revelation. Their indulgence requires greater and greater intensities of validation for the same levels of gratification. Without the traction provided by Gospel sod, they slip backward toward the precipice of destruction. It is our restraint that conditions our faith to believe in the miracle of the birth of Christ, to experience the thrill of being spiritually begotten of Him, and to have our hearts changed through faith on His name. Because we carry the Christmas season in our hearts, He is ever before us, on our right hand, and on our left, and His angels are round about us, to bear us up. (See D&C 84:88).

> Christmas
> is the season of
> the year when we pause
> in our frenzied pursuit of
> temporal treasure to brush
> away the cobwebs from
> our minds, stretch our
> spiritual muscles, and
> crane our necks
> to look up to
> heaven.

Those who are stiff-necked lack the pliancy, flexibility, and perspective of faith. Stubbornness prevents them from looking up to Heavenly Father for guidance, over to priesthood leaders for counsel, around to seek out those in need, and down in an attitude of humility. The Christmas story has the power to soften our telestial tendencies, assuage our secular skepticism, and blur the lines distinguishing mortality from eternity. It leaves us eager to respond to the questions that loom before us all: "What think ye of Christmas?" and "Whose Son was born that day?"

> Christmas is
> the season of the year
> when we stand revealed
> before the Maker and
> Fashioner of the
> universe.

We cannot lie to Him, for we write the record of our lives in the sinews of our bodies and on the tablets of our minds. In a coming day, both will be unfolded before God and angels, who will read those records as easily as we read a book. At that moment, through the power of the Atonement, our vision will be energized with infinite perspective, and we will experience a pulsing stream of inspiration whose mighty flow will have no temporal or spatial boundary. We will be swept up by quickening currents into the direct experience of a holy communion with God. His thoughts will have somehow become our thoughts, and His ways will have become our ways. (See Isaiah 55:8). We will be caught up in a rapture where legions of angels will confirm that the universe has become "a machine for the making of gods." (Henri Bergson, "Two Sources of Morality and Religion," 1932).

> Christmas is the
> season of the year
> when we draw freely
> from an inexhaustible
> fountain of living water.

When we harden our hearts against the glad tidings of the message of salvation, the flow from that well will slow to a trickle to leave us defenseless against the suffocating desert winds of the devil. Christmas helps us to put all the pieces of the puzzle of life together. It answers the question Alice posed to the Cheshire Cat: "Would you please tell me which way I ought to go from here?" Replied the cat: "That depends a good deal on where you want to go." "I admit," responded Alice, "I don't much care where." Said the cat: "Then it doesn't matter which way you go." "Just so I go somewhere!" cried Alice. "Oh," responded the cat, "you are sure to do that, if you walk far enough." (Lewis Carroll, "Alice's Adventures in Wonderland").

Christmas
is the season of the year
when we resolve to achieve
fluency in the language
of the scriptures that
testify of Christ.

Only when we have paid the price, will the words of the prophets flow easily and poetically to our minds. Fluency will come after practice that is manifested by memorization, recitation, individual and cooperative study, comparison with companion scriptures, and expansion of understanding by critical analysis of supportive commentaries. Faith, fasting, and prayer at Christmas time and throughout the year will lead to insight, intuition, inspiration, discernment, and revelation.

Christmas
is the season
of the year when,
although we don't think
about it too often, we have a
wonderful opportunity to put the
Fall in proper perspective. "For as in
Adam all die, even so in Christ
shall all be made alive."
(1 Corinthians 15:22).

When the Fall is considered in conjunction with the birth, ministry, atonement, death, and resurrection of Christ, it is clear that all are part of God's Plan of Eternal Progression. When Lehi wrote that "Adam fell that men might be, and men are that they might have joy," He understood that we are "spirit, the elements are eternal, and spirit and element, inseparably connected, receive a fullness of joy." (2 Nephi 2:25 & D&C 93:33).

> Christmas is the season of the year when we can feel safe in our knowledge of God.

In the midst of persecution that would seven years later take his life, William Tyndall confidently wrote of his testimony of Christ, that "it declares that we are safe already, and certifies our hearts and makes us feel that our faith is right and that God's spirit is in us." (William Tyndall, "Obedience," p. 117). Knowledge received through the exercise of faith is the mortar that binds together the building blocks of conversion. A wise Teacher counseled that knowledge is received by faith. (See D&C 26:2). He taught: "As all have not faith, seek ye diligently and teach one another words of wisdom; yea, seek ye out of the best books words of wisdom; seek learning, even by study and also by faith." (D&C 88:118).

Christmas
is the season
of the year when "the
heavenly star, its rays afar,
on every land is throwing; and
shall not cease, 'til holy peace
in all the earth is growing."
("With Wondering Awe").

When that light has penetrated every clime, every man shall be his own priest, and every woman her own priestess, to whom the Lord God shall incline His ear. They shall prophesy and shall dream dreams. There shall be no "confession in the ear. For neither the Apostles nor they that followed many hundred years after knew of any such whispering." (William Tyndall, "Obedience," p. 120).

Christmas is
the season of the year
when "to the earth (the star
above Bethlehem) gave great
light; and so it continued
both day and night."
("The First Noel").

"And behold, there shall a new star arise, such an one as ye never have beheld; and this also shall be a sign unto you." (Helaman 14:5). Zoroastrian priests beheld the light and recognized its significance. Making haste, they traveled to Jerusalem after the Savior's birth, and inquired of Herod: "Where is he that is born King of the Jews? For we have seen his star in the east, and are come to worship him." (Matthew 2:2).

> Christmas is
> the season of the
> year when we are all
> "amazed, and wonder"
> at the gift of God that
> was so freely given.
> (Helaman 14:7)

Christmas confounds "the worldly wise, who are enemies to the wisdom of God, who are deep and profound wells without water, who are clouds without moisture of rain, and who are natural souls without the Spirit of God." (William Tyndall, "Obedience," p. 116). To the most hardened skeptics of the birth of His Son, the signs and wonders of the season are God's own testimony.

Christmas is the season of the year when we are touched to the very core of our spiritual center, when we feel in our hearts that we have consented unto the law of God.

Under such circumstances, "we feel ourselves meek, patient, courteous, and merciful to our neighbours, altered and fashioned like unto Christ. Why, then, should we doubt but that God hath forgiven us, and chosen us, and put his Spirit in us?" (William Tyndale, "Obedience," p. 118).

> Christmas is the season
> of the year when we listen to
> the sound of trumpets speaking
> to us from the heavens, and
> we hear their clarion call,
> not with our ears, but
> with our hearts.

Sometimes, the gulf between the secular and the sacred cannot be bridged with profane speech. When the Lord spoke to His Father in the presence of the Nephite Saints, "so great and marvelous were the words which he prayed, that they cannot be written, neither can they be uttered by man." (3 Nephi 19:34). Nevertheless, the spiritual preparation of the multitude permitted them to receive those things, and so "they did understand in their hearts the words which he prayed." (2 Nephi 19:33).

Christmas is the season of the year when it seems to be most appropriate to ask the Lord: "Bless all the dear children in Thy tender care, and fit us for heaven to live with Thee there." ("Away in a Manger").

In Zarahemla, the Saints brought their children to the Savior, that He might minister to them. After taking them "one by one, (He) blessed them, and prayed unto the Father for them." (3 Nephi 17:21). The Spirit was overwhelming and as the multitude raised their eyes, "they saw the heavens open, and they saw angels descending out of heaven, as it were, in the midst of fire; and they came down and encircled those little ones about, and they were encircled about with fire. And the angels did minister unto them." (3 Nephi 17:24). Truly, they were "one, the Children of Christ, and heirs to the kingdom of God." (4 Nephi 1:3 & 17).

> Christmas is the
> season of the year when
> we ponder how the morning
> stars were mustered out of
> heaven to bear witness
> of the holy birth."
> (See Job 38:7).

God and the morning stars are able to see at once, the beginning and the end. The morning stars witnessed the birth of the Savior now and forever, and they were, and are, and forever will be singing together and shouting for joy. (See Job 38:7). As Alma explained to Corianton: "All is as one day with God, and time only is measured unto men." (Alma 40:8). Einstein was right; time is relative. Joseph Smith said: "The great Jehovah contemplated the whole of the events connected with the earth ... before it rolled into existence, or ever 'the morning stars sang together' for joy; the past, the present, and the future were and are, with him, one eternal now." (Teachings," p. 220). The Savior exists in the past, present, and future tense; He is "the Great I AM, Alpha and Omega." (D&C 38:1). His "course is one eternal round, the same today as yesterday, and forever." (D&C 35:1).

Christmas is the season of the year when the invitation is extended to "come unto Christ, and (to) be perfected in Him." (Moroni 10:32).

We are invited to move off Santa's telestial terrain, and to grasp the horns of sanctuary where the "covenants and ordinances will fill us with faith as a living fire. In a day of desolating sickness, scorched earth, barren wastes, sickening plagues, disease, destruction, and death, we as a people will rest in the shade of trees, we will drink from the cooling fountains. We will abide in places of refuge from the storm; we will mount up as on the wings of eagles; we will be lifted out of an insane and evil world. We will be as fair as the sun and clear as the moon." (Vaughn Featherstone).

Christmas is the season of the year when we marvel at how long the earth has lain in a "deep and dreamless sleep," while "the silent stars go by." ("O Little Town of Bethlehem").

But now, as we awaken and arise, we are assured that "no unhallowed hand can stop the work from progressing; persecutions may rage, mobs may combine, armies may assemble, calumny may defame, but the truth of God will go forth boldly, nobly, and independent, until it has penetrated every continent, visited every clime, swept every country, and sounded in every ear, 'til the purposes of God shall be accomplished and the Great Jehovah shall say 'The work is done.'" (Joseph Smith, "The Wentworth Letter," H.C. 4:540).

Christmas is the season of the year when "truth, heaven born, in its beauty and glory is marching triumphantly over the world." ("Awake and Arise").

To paraphrase Tom Paine: Christmas is a time that will try our souls. The summer soldier and the sunshine patriot will, at this season of the year, shrink from their worship of God, but those who do so now, intensely feel Hs love. Ignorance of the meaning of Christmas, like hell, is not easily conquered; yet we have this consolation with us, that the harder our divine commission, the more glorious the triumph. What we obtain too cheap, we esteem too lightly. 'Tis dearness only that gives everything its value. Heaven knows how to put a proper price upon its goods; and it would be strange, indeed, if so celestial an article as a real appreciation of the significance of the birth of the Savior should not be highly rated. (See "The Crisis", 12/23/1776).

> Christmas
> is the season of
> the year when we are
> quickened by the Spirit
> to see the glory of
> the Coming of
> the Lord.

When, in just 24 days, George Frideric Handel created the 259 pages of musical score that comprise "The Messiah", the notes came to him so quickly that he could barely keep up, as he furiously scratched out the oratorio on whatever paper was handy. After he had written the "Hallelujah Chorus" in a fervor of divine inspiration, he exclaimed that he had seen all heaven before him. At the end of the manuscript, in acknowledgement of his own puny efforts, he wrote the letters "SDG" that stood for "Soli Deo Gloria" or "To God alone the glory."

> Christmas
> is the season
> of the year that
> helps us appreciate
> that the divine design
> of the ordinance of the
> Sacrament is to light
> the world.

Partaking of the emblems of Christ blesses us with a continuing endowment of the Holy Spirit, which is enough to bring us into the presence of God. It is as if we are kneeling at the manger to adore and worship the Newborn King.

Christmas is the season of the year when we can be sure that He knows when we are sleeping and He knows when we're awake.

Paper and ink and even tablets of metal, stone, or clay may or may not survive the ravages of time, but God will be able to read the record of our lives engraved in our very sinews. For Him who created us, that tapestry woven into our souls may be read as easily as any printed text. Our Heavenly Father knows when we've been bad or good, so we need to be good for goodness' sake! (John Frederick Coots and Haven Gillespie, "Santa Claus is Coming to Town").

Christmas is the
season of the year when
latter-day shepherds who
are tending their flocks cannot
help but brush up against the veil.
The Spirit cannot be restrained,
and sometimes it even maketh
their bones to quake while it
maketh itself manifest.
(See D&C 85:6).

As it does so, they will hear the music of heavenly choirs and discern the voices of angelic messengers testifying that the Son of God has come in righteousness "to declare the glad tidings of great joy." (Mosiah 3:3). "In the dark recesses of memory, in unbidden suggestions, in trains of thought unwittingly pursued, in multiplied waves and currents all at once flashing and rushing, in dreams that cannot be laid to rest, in the force of instinct, in the obscure, but certain, intuitions of the spiritual life, they will have glimpses of a great tide of life ebbing and flowing, rippling and roiling and beating about where they cannot see it." (E.S. Dallas).

> Christmas is
> the season of the year
> when "we tingle," not due to
> the frost in the air, but because
> of "the consciousness of our
> kinship with the Infinite."
> (David O. McKay).

If we reject that intimate association with the Divine, we damage our eternal selves, for as the Lord warned, "in an hour when ye think not the summer shall be past, and the harvest ended, and your souls not saved." (D&C 45:2). Whether we acknowledge it or not, every second of every day, we are one tick of the clock closer to "the undiscovered country, from whose bourn no traveler returns." (Shakespeare, Hamlet, Act 3, Scene 1). Christmas invites us to make every one of those seconds count for something.

> Christmas
> is the season of
> the year when pearls
> are cast before those who
> persist in coveting the
> treasures of the
> earth.

Imitations of the divine model have been fashioned by telestial tailors for those whose undisciplined minds are easily swayed by the siren song of Satan. The master deceiver knows that unprincipled character will crumble in the face of traumatizing temptations, counterfeit currency, and unearned blessings that have been cleverly disguised as tantalizing treats. Those who focus on the idols of the day are more prone to ask: "What did you get for Christmas?" rather than "What did you give for Christmas?"

Christmas is the season of the year when we try to emulate the Wise Men of old.

Heber J. Grant said those who are truly wise "are striving, working, and trying to the best of their ability to improve day by day." He said: "We are in the line of our duty, if we are seeking to remedy our own defects, if we are so living that we can ask for light, for knowledge, for intelligence, and above all, for His Spirit that we may overcome weakness. Then, I can tell you, we are in the straight and narrow path that leads to life eternal." (C.R., 4/1909).
Then, with the Wise Men of old, we will be following the Christmas Star to Bethlehem.

> Christmas is the season of the year when the influence of the Holy Ghost seems to be unrestrained. His invitation is sent throughout all the world, to come unto the Savior to "partake of His goodness; and He denieth none that come unto Him ... and all are alike unto God." (2 Nephi 26:33).

Paul observed of the Athenians, who were not so very different from us, that they were inclined to bow down before unknown gods, whom, therefore, they ignorantly worshipped. What matters is that our celebration of Christmas better prepares us to stand independently as witnesses of the true and living God. It was with this in mind that Paul bore testimony to those gathered at Mars Hill: "Him I declare ... unto you." (Acts 17:23, see 1 Thessalonians 1:9).

> Christmas
> is the season
> of the year that is a
> good time for others
> of God's children
> to be introduced
> to the Gospel
> of Jesus
> Christ.

This may not be easy, because as Dallin Oaks observed: "Salvation is not a cheap experience." We need Christmas in our arsenal as we engage the forces of Babylon on the field of battle. Our witness of Christ is nurtured by our understanding of His ministry, but it is grounded in Bethlehem. Because there is "a great division among the people" regarding how they celebrate Christmas, "the time has come for a day of choosing." (D&C 105:35),

> Christmas is
> the season of the
> year when it is all too
> easy to become preoccupied
> with Santa Claus by focusing
> on his sleigh full of toys
> and treats rather than
> on the solemnities
> of eternity

We will receive very little divine tutorial training if we look in the wrong places for communication from the heavens. In days past, the prophets repeatedly warned Israel against dalliances with astrologers, exorcists, familiar spirits, magicians, sorcerers, witches, and against participating in divinations and enchantments. Today, during the Christmas season, we are all too familiar with equivalent distractions that have been repackaged but not repurposed. Their design remains the same: to dilute His doctrine until it is indistinguishable from secular caricatures of the celestial model, to divert us from the worship of Jesus Christ by putting a Santa Claus in every department store, and to discourage the commemoration of His holy day by celebrating it as just another holiday.

Christmas is the season of the year when parking stalls at the mall are full of cars that should be competing for spaces at church.

Stripes on the pavement define patterns of subtle self-indulgence, neglect of spiritual responsibilities, and even loss of divine protection, when they accommodate cars on the Sabbath. Long ago, Alexis de Tocqueville wrote: "I sought for the greatness and genius of America, but not until I went to her churches and heard her pulpits aflame with righteousness did I understand the secret of her genius and her power. America is great because she is good, and if she ever ceases to be good, she will cease to be great."

Christmas
is the season
of the year when
small children wait
in long lines for a
chance to sit on
Santa's lap.

Soberly, we remember how Jesus ministered to the Nephite children. He took them "one by one, and blessed them, and prayed unto the Father for them ... And they saw the heavens open, and they saw angels descending out of heaven ... and they were encircled about with fire; and the angels did minister unto them." (3 Nephi 17:21-24).

> Christmas
> is the season of
> the year when Frosty
> the Snowman competes
> with the Nativity Scene
> for attention in
> our yards.

"Away in a manger, no crib for his bed, the little Lord Jesus laid down His sweet head." ("Away in a Manger"). If we maintain our focus at Christmas time, the pathway to the summit of our worship will climb steadily to the hill country of Judea, and all the way to Bethlehem. We celebrate Christmas there because that little town has become a celestial beacon to the world; a silver city where we can join angels and cherubim, singing Hosannas to His Holy name.

Christmas is the season
of the year when we realize
that our familiarity with the
circumstances surrounding
the birth of the Savior
introduces us to a
larger view of
life.

Christmas is the culmination of the annual cycle of our mortal experience; it gathers up our trials and tribulations and even our broken dreams, and quietly sets them aside in a corner, to be dealt with later, to be surrendered to the Savior, and ultimately to be forgotten. It answers the questions that trouble our spirits, and it empowers us to comprehend with greater clarity the solemnities of eternity. As our understanding expands, and we see more clearly with the eye of faith, we establish a sure footing on the bedrock of unchanging Gospel principles.

Christmas
is the season of
the year when we are
showered with types and
shadows that orient us to
the Savior: trees, ornaments,
lights, candy canes, stars, bells,
and packages wrapped with gaily
colored ribbons and bows. We need
to remember that they are only
symbols, inviting us to dig
more deeply into their
significance.

In His ministry, the Savior frequently used symbols. He talked of lost sheep, mustard seeds, fig trees, olive branches, pearls of great price, hens, chickens, birds, flowers, and foxes, bread and water, and bitter cups. He told Moses: "All things have their likeness, and all things are created and made to bear record of me." (Moses 6:63). Christmas is no exception. In reality "earth is crammed with heaven, and every common bush with fire of God. But only those who see take off their shoes. The rest stand around picking blackberries." (Elizabeth Barrett Browning). So too, was that first Nativity crammed with heaven, and with the fire of God.

Christmas is
the season of the year
when we gratefully thank our
Heavenly Father for bringing the
gift of joy into the world. We also
acknowledge that there are forces
of good and evil at play, and
that wickedness is the polar
opposite of happiness.
(See Alma 41:10).

Those who cannot embrace the spirit of the season must surely experience despair, which is the feeling of hopelessness that is the natural consequence of disobedience. It "cometh because of iniquity." (Moroni 10:22). Every law of God has both a blessing and a punishment affixed to it. When law is obeyed, a blessing is given that results in happiness or joy. When law is disobeyed, punishment is given that results in unhappiness or misery. Beside the carousel of life, Christmas is our brass ring; our golden ticket. It is our winning lottery number, redeemable for unspeakable joy in the Kingdom of our Father.

> Christmas is
> the season of the
> year when we feel a
> kinship with those who
> were specifically raised
> up by God from before
> their birth to be humble
> understudies to the
> Great Jehovah.

"The Lord hath called me from the womb" wrote Isaiah, "from the bowels of my mother hath he made mention of my name." (Isaiah 49:1). "Once or twice in a thousand years, perhaps a dozen times since mortal man became of dust a living soul, an event of such transcendent import occurs that neither heaven nor earth is ever thereafter the same. Once or twice in a score of generations, the hand from heaven clasps the hand on earth in perfect fellowship, the divine drama unfolds, and the whole course of mortal events changes." (Bruce R. McConkie, C.R., 10/75). Such have been the circumstances of those who have been raised up to usher in dispensations of the Gospel, and to bear witness of the birth of the Son of God.

Christmas is the season of the year that invites us to come in from the cold; from the estrangement of the world to enjoy the warmth of the Gospel.

Those who accept the invitation will find a refuge from confusion and doubt. They will discover their "instructor in principle, doctrine, and righteousness; their guide in matters of faith and morals." (B.H. Roberts, H.C., 1:393). They will "come out of the world, leaving the loneliness of a fallen creation to enter the realm of divine experience. They will forsake the orphanage of spiritual alienation, to be received into the family and household of the Lord Jesus Christ." ("Doctrinal Commentary on The Book of Mormon," 4:202).

Christmas is
the season of the
year that gives us an
opportunity to prove to
the world that charity
is a reflection of
our true nature.

Because "charity is the pure love of Christ, it endureth forever, and whoso is found possessed of it at the last day, it shall be well with him." (Moroni 7:47). As a bellwether of service, Christmas prepares us to be comfortable when the day arrives that we will be surrounded by His all-encompassing love.

> Christmas is the season of the year when our potential may be quickened by the influence of the Spirit.

The Holy Ghost energizes our capabilities with a vitality we would not otherwise enjoy. As Bagheera, the powerfully built black panther confided to Mowgli the man-cub: "I had never seen the jungle. They fed me behind bars from an iron pan until one night I felt that I was Bagheera the Panther, and no man's plaything, and I broke the lock with one blow of my paw and came away." (Rudyard Kipling, "The Jungle Book", p. 26).

> Christmas is the season of the year that lends itself to the invitation to stand in holy places.

Hallowed halls have more to do with how we live than where we conduct our daily affairs. A holy place, then, is anywhere we enjoy the presence of the Spirit. "Who shall ascend into the hill of the Lord" at Christmas time, asked the Psalmist, "or who shall stand in his holy place? He that hath clean hands, and a pure heart; who hath not lifted up his soul unto vanity, nor sworn deceitfully. He shall receive the blessing from the Lord, and righteousness from the God of his salvation." (Psalms 24:3-5).

Christmas is the
season of the year when
shepherds quake at the sight of
glories streaming from heaven
afar, and of a Heavenly host
proclaiming hallelujah, in
their joyous praise
of God.

"Sing unto the Lord", exclaimed Isaiah, "for he hath done excellent things; this is known in all the earth. Cry out and shout, thou inhabitant of Zion; for great is the Holy One of Israel." (Isaiah 12:5-6). Christmas introduces us to a ladder that has been set up on the earth, the top of which reaches all the way to heaven. (See Genesis 28:12). As we ascend rung by rung, we will see lightnings and mountains smoking, and hear thunderings and the voices of trumpets speaking to us in a musical language that is inarticulate, indescribable, and yet irrefutable. (See Exodus 20:18, & Hebrews 12:19)

Christmas is the season of the year when "Lo! The days are hastening on, by prophets seen of old. When with the ever-circling years, shall come the time foretold." ("It Came Upon a Midnight Clear").

His disciples patiently acknowledge the Lord's timetable, while the world insists on instant satisfaction and immediate gratification through the natural senses. Disciples remove the latchets from their shoes in the presence of burning bushes, while Babylon remains pre-occupied with the occult, and with magic, diviners and soothsayers, rolling the dice and dreaming of the riches that will be hers if only her lucky number comes up. Disciples stand in holy places and are not moved, while Babylon appropriates money for military preparedness in a false sense of security that is curiously supported by the doctrine of Mutually Assured Destruction. It's a Mad, Mad World that needs the Second Coming as much as it needed the first Christmas.

> Christmas
> is the season
> of the year when we
> look up at the night sky
> and stare in wonder at the
> same stars twinkling in the
> heavens that looked down
> upon Joseph, Mary, and
> the Christ Child.

The light we now see shining down from above may have been traveling through space for +/- 2,020 years (about 12,000,000,000,000,000 miles), ever since it left its host star. At least some of the starlight we see today, then, may have burst forth from its home system at the time of the Savior's birth. Heavenly Father has provided a way for us to directly participate in the spectacular light show of the Nativity itself. Who knows but that it may have been us to whom the Savior referred, when He asked Job: "Where wast thou when I laid the foundations of the earth? ... When the morning stars sang together, and all the sons of God shouted for joy? (Job 38:4&7).

> Christmas
> is the season of
> the year that makes
> it easier for "the law to
> be written in our hearts
> by the Spirit of God."
> (William Tyndall).

"Blessed is the man (whose) delight is in the law of the Lord. (For) he shall be like a tree planted by the rivers of water, that bringeth forth his fruit in his season; his leaf also shall not wither; and whatsoever he doeth shall prosper. The ungodly are not so: but are like the chaff which the wind driveth away. Therefore, the ungodly shall not stand in the judgment, nor sinners in the congregation of the righteous. For the Lord knoweth the way of the righteous: but the way of the ungodly shall perish." (Psalms 1:1-6).

> Christmas is the season of the year when the poverty of the scene at the Nativity teaches us where we should place our priorities.

The Savior taught: "Lay not up for yourselves treasures upon earth, where moth and rust doth corrupt, and where thieves break through and steal. But lay up for yourselves treasures in heaven." (Matthew 6:19-20). Babylon celebrates the holidays by worshipping the almighty dollar, secularizing the sacred, and trading in counterfeit currency. Our Heavenly Father, on the other hand, uses Christmas to teach life lessons, wherein the wealthy are abased that the poor might be exalted. This is one of the hardest things for the unconverted to understand.

Christmas
is the season of the
year when our focus on
the one is underscored by
the simplicity of the scene
in the Nativity, where our
attention, with that of
Joseph and Mary,
is riveted on
the Christ
Child.

We are reminded that much of what we do at Christmas is scaffolding. As we seek to build our relationship with the Savior, we must not confuse the scaffolding with its true purpose. Our affection for the Christ Child must be a more pure and enduring substance; we must be willing, as He was during His ministry, to leave the ninety nine, to save one lost sheep. (See Matthew 18:12). As Gordon B. Hinckley cautioned, we cannot hope to save a man or a woman on Sunday, if during the week we are a complacent witness to the destruction of their soul.

Christmas is the season of the year when the heat from chestnuts that are roasting by an open fire reminds us to be aflame with faith.

"His word was in mine heart as a burning fire shut up in my bones, and I was weary with forbearing, and I could not stay." (Jeremiah 20:9). Fire and smoke remind us of the glory of celestial realms, as well as of the splendor that surrounded the Nativity on that first Christmas morning. "God Almighty Himself dwells in eternal fire. Flesh and blood cannot go there, for all corruption is devoured by that fire." (Joseph Smith, "Teachings," p. 367).

Christmas is the
season of the year when
our prayers seem to more
easily flow to "our Father,
which art in heaven."
(Matthew 6:9).

In the prototypical Lord's Prayer, He emphasized that His Father is in a holy place where Santa can never trespass. His celestial throne is completely secure. It is a sea of glass, a reservoir of inspiration, and a source of revelation. Our prayers illuminate a path that traces its way to a dwelling built to last for all eternity. God's presence is the ultimate expression of security; in Him there "is no variableness, neither shadow of turning." (James 1:17). In heavenly realms, there is no ambiguity, but only the clarity of a flood of unimaginably intense light. Christmas provides us with an opportunity to have our own "Road to Damascus" experience. Of that consummate encounter with the Spirit, Paul simply said: "Our God is a consuming fire." (Hebrews 12:29).

*Christmas
is the season of
the year that helps us to
conquer our winter doldrums;
to see with the eye of faith
in the light of days that
are finally growing
longer.*

Throughout the year, our sponge is wrung nearly dry as we seek to cool our feverish foreheads with living water. What a blessing it is to know that there is light at the end of a long tunnel of darkness; that every December there is a haven and a place of refuge from the turmoil of the world. At Christmas, we reaffirm that life has purpose and direction, and we quietly rededicate ourselves to the Savior. He shows us how to increase in wisdom and in stature, not only around the holidays, but also throughout the year.

> Christmas
> is the season of the
> year that invites us to
> focus on one brief, shining
> moment in Judea 2,000 years
> ago, when the veil became
> transparent, and the wide
> expanse of eternity was
> opened up to the view
> of the children
> of men.

When the veil is removed from our eyes, we will find ourselves awash in a panoramic comprehension of spiritual certainty. Gone will be inconsistent glimmers of light. With crystal clarity, we will see from the time we were uncreated intelligence, through our development as spirit children of our Heavenly Father, on to mortality, and finally to our reunion with Him in the resurrection. "Knowledge will rush in from all quarters; it will come to us like the light that flows from the sun, penetrating every part, informing the Spirit, and giving understanding concerning ten thousand things at the same time; and our minds will be capable of receiving and retaining all." (Orson Pratt, J.D., 2:246).

Christmas is
the season of the year
when we learn from the Lord's
humble birth that real poverty is
untested potential which is the
result of self-imposed
limitations.

Too often, we hear "The sky's the limit," but that is not so. If we learn to keep our faces oriented toward heaven, we will rise to new heights, and the Christmas season will become the antidote to secular vertigo. From the vantage point of the spiritual stratosphere, we will look down at what we had thought were telestial stumbling-blocks. When we figuratively unwrap these gifts from God, we will discover their magical potential to become celestial stepping-stones. As we hop from one to another, we will discover that they have been strategically placed by God to help us to reach the stability of a far shore upon which we will find Him waiting to welcome us Home.

Christmas is
the season of the year
when we affirm our faith in
the immortality of our souls,
because within ourselves there
exist inexplicable longings
that relentlessly tug at
us from the other
side of the
veil.

"Who are these children coming down like gentle rain through darkened skies, with glory trailing from their feet as they go, and endless promise in their eyes? Who are these young ones growing tall, growing strong, like silver trees against the storm; who will not bend with the wind or the change, but stand to fight the world alone? These are the few, the warriors saved for Saturday; to come the last day of the world. These are the strong, the warriors rising in their might to win the battle raging in the hearts of men," at Christmas-time. (Doug Stewart, "Saturday's Warrior").

Christmas
is the season
of the year when
nature's rhythms are
felt by those who
are in harmony
with eternity.

The veil is almost transparent as our powers expand and we experience the glittering facets of the life of the Spirit. The Gospel sets us free so that we may be more creative and encourages us to be more creative so that we may enjoy greater freedom. It is the perfect law of liberty.

Christmas is
the season of the
year when we burst
beyond the fetters
of our perceived
limitations.

Whenever our priorities are out of order, we lose the power to bring about positive change, but when the Savior is the focus of our lives, the clarity of our vision unleashes untapped potential. Christmas is a lens that focuses our perspective to become crystal clear, enabling us to comprehend and build upon the principles of perfection.

Christmas is the season of the year when skyrocketing credit card balances are eclipsed only by our greater debt to our Savior.

"Each of us lives on a kind of spiritual credit. One day the account will be closed, and a settlement demanded. However casually we may view it now, when that day comes, and the foreclosure is imminent, we will look around in restless agony for someone, anyone, to help us. And by eternal law, mercy cannot be extended save there be one who is both willing and able to assume our debt, and pay the price, and arrange the terms of our redemption." (Boyd Packer, "Ensign," 4/1977).

> Christmas is the
> season of the year that
> invites us to pause in our
> perpetual efforts to exhaust
> ourselves in trivial pursuits;
> it urges us to step back, and
> to take a cleansing breath of
> refreshing and reinvigorating
> celestial air; to increase the
> spiritual element saturation
> of our blood to 100%.

The best way to prepare for God's Rest is to follow with exactness The Plan of Happiness. When we internalize its provisions, we will enter into the peace born of a settled conviction of the truth. When we are obedient to celestial principles and have gained a perfect testimony of the divinity of the work, we will no longer suffer from fear, doubt, the religious turmoil of the world, or from the vagaries of men. Christmas is our Tai Chi; we embrace the holidays with a series of gentle exercises, as we stretch ourselves physically, mentally, and spiritually. Each posture flows seamlessly into the next in a constant motion. With a focus on the Savior, we retain fluidity with nature, and harmony with the unseen world.

Christmas
is the season of
the year when the love
of the Savior forms a bridge
between the world of everyday
and the Land of Promise, whose
well-watered trees are laden with
figs, dates, and olives, and whose
streets are paved with our
gilded hopes and our
jewel-encrusted
dreams.

Because "fools rush in where angels fear to tread," Christmas has been designed to be enjoyed in time, that we might be better prepared for eternity. (Alexander Pope, "An Essay on Criticism"). The season exposes us to the sensory delights of fragrance, sound, form, and color, as well as to gratitude, loyalty, and appreciation. It is selflessness, helpful, and forgiving, and introduces us to love and compassion; to truth, beauty, and goodness, and to the realm of human growth and transcendence. It is a perfect vehicle to get us up and moving on the pathway to perfection.

Christmas
is the season
of the year that
warms our hearts
before the living
fire of faith.

"We as a people will rest in the shade of trees, and we will drink from the cooling fountains. We will abide in places of refuge from the storm; we will mount up as on eagles' wings, and we will be lifted out of an insane and evil world. We will be as fair as the sun and clear as the moon. Our children will bow down at the feet of the Savior and worship Him as the Lord of lords, the King of kings. They will bathe His feet with their tears and He will bless them." (Vaughn Featherstone, Utah South Stake, 4/1987).

Christmas
is the season
of the year when
it is easy to buy into
the fiction that we are
deserving of the comfort
of our hearth and home. At
these times, we need to be on
our guard to avoid drawing
hasty conclusions to our
own advantage.

"If we were stronger, we might be less tenderly treated. If we were braver, we might be sent, with far less help, to defend far more desperate posts in the great battle." (C.S. Lewis, "The World's Last Night" p. 10-11).

Christmas is the
season of the year
when we may express our
appreciation to our Father in
Heaven for the most wonderful
Gift of all. Rather than sending
text messages or an email, tagging
Him in a Facebook post, mentioning
Him on Twitter, or even dropping a
thank you note in the mail, He
values simple expressions of
gratitude that are woven
into the fabric of our
heart-felt prayers.

"Gratitude is not only the greatest of virtues, but the parent of all the others." (Cicero). When we cultivate feelings of gratitude, a wonderful transformation of our outlook on life occurs. We are not grateful because we are happy; we are happy because we are grateful. With gratitude in our hearts, good outweighs evil, love overpowers jealousy, light drives out darkness, knowledge banishes ignorance, and humility displaces self-sufficiency. Courtesy overwhelms rudeness, appreciation overcomes bitterness, abundance supersedes poverty, and well-being supplants weakness. Expressions of gratitude make life's experiences exhilarating.

Christmas is the season of the year when, almost without effort, a divine perspective is nurtured that seems to come to us quite naturally. Salutations of "Merry Christmas!" easily flow from our lips and leave us with the taste of honey on the tips of our tongues.

Even when our own plans go awry, we cling to the promise that "the Lord shall come, and his recompense shall be with him, and he shall reward every man." (D&C 56:19). Our Christmas thanksgiving propels us on our passage heavenward, but we ought not allow it to lull us into a sense of complacency, for "our Father in Heaven will refresh us on the journey through life with some pleasant inns, but he will not encourage us to mistake them for home." (C.S. Lewis, "The Problem of Pain").

> Christmas
> is the season of
> year when we try harder
> to keep the commandments.
> We strive to endure to the end
> in righteousness, and embrace
> the principles that pertain
> to happiness.

Our worship must not be superficial or ritualistic. It must generate feeling, emotion, and the spiritual horsepower to create traction on the slippery sod of secularism. Christmas provides context, and establishes spontaneity, enthusiasm, and vitality in our worship, which is evidence of the powerful relationship that can exist between ourselves and God. It arises out of the deepest convictions of our soul, and not from a desire simply to go along with the crowd.

> Christmas is the season of year when we resolve to repent because we have caught the vision of our Father, Who sent His Firstborn Son into the world with one purpose in mind; to redeem us from the Fall.

Without repentance, our misdeeds of the past would forever extort our best efforts now, hold our future hostage, and as a result, thwart the great Plan of Salvation. As Nephi exclaimed: "Rejoice, O my heart, and give place no more for the enemy of my soul. Do not anger again because of mine enemies. Do not slacken my strength because of mine afflictions. Rejoice, O my heart." (2 Nephi 4:28-30).

> Christmas is the season of the year when our fears seem to disperse like dew before the morning sun, and our dreams become our destiny.

Still, the poet asked: "Why is it whenever I reach for the sky to climb aboard cloud nine, it evaporates and rains upon my dreams? Is it a matter of science, or simply a matter of fact, that not even a cloud with a silver lining can hold the weight of our dreams without some precipitation? I think I've found the answer to this dilemma. Keep on reaching for the sky, but don't forget your umbrella." (Susan Stephenson, "Cloud Nine").

Christmas is the season of the year when we acknowledge the might, majesty, power, priesthood dominion, and authority of Him Who is "the blessed and only Potentate, the King of kings and Lord of lords, to whom be honor and power everlasting." (J.S.T. 1 Timothy 6:15).

We are in awe that He would entrust His servants with the responsibility to administer His earthly kingdom. They are weak and simple and unlearned. Of themselves, they can do nothing, but in the strength of the Lord, they cannot fail. It is His power that sustains and guides them. Their position, status, and divine commission are no different from that of His servants of old. Especially at Christmas, we hope to be able to respond to the question: "Whom say ye that I am?" as did Peter. Without a moment's hesitation, he declared: "Thou art the Christ, the Son of the Living God." (Matthew 16:15-16).

> Christmas is the season of the year when every requirement of citizenship is waived and all the world is invited to partake of the blessings that freely flow out of the little town of Bethlehem.

Christmas is celebrated throughout the world, because the pivotal experiences of mortality must remain neutralized until every nation, kindred, tongue, and people has developed a relationship with the Savior. (See Revelation 14:6). For eternal life is to know the only true God, and Jesus Christ whom He sent. (See John 17:3). Joseph Smith said that there are but a very few beings in the world who understand rightly the nature of God, and that if we do not understand His character, we cannot comprehend ourselves. (See "Teachings," p. 343).

Christmas
is the season
of the year when
an alarming trend
is reversed; when the
world is not taken into
the Gospel, but it is the
other way around, and
the Gospel is taken
into the world.

The standard of the Lord's Church must remain steadfast, because "it would be impossible for us to become popular with the world, because then all hell would want to join us." (Ezra Taft Benson, C.R., 4/1969).

Christmas is the season of the year that teaches us that we should be content with our circumstances and at peace with our lot in life; that we should be grateful for what we have been given, rather than frustrated because of what we have been denied.

"Little people, like you and me, if our prayers are sometimes granted beyond all hope and probability, had better not draw hasty conclusions to our own advantage." (C.S. Lewis, "The World's Last Night," p. 10-11).

Christmas is
the season of the
year when God's gifts
are largely overlooked in
a frenzied quest for the
fine-twined linens
and the baubles
of Babylon.

The real gifts of Christmas include baptism, (a covenant of salvation), the companionship of the Holy Ghost, (a covenant of justification), the Sacrament, (a covenant of sanctification), and celestial marriage, (a covenant of exaltation).

> Christmas is
> the season of the
> year when the witness
> of Jesus Christ is offered
> as a gift without money and
> without price, that His restored
> Gospel might light the world
> as from a clean, renewable,
> and inexhaustible Source
> of energy.

It is only necessary to pay the price of a broken heart and a contrite spirit to discover the merits of its treasures and the relevance of its messages. These include a wealth of doctrine imbedded in a historical matrix that touches on reality in a thousand different ways. The word of God has allowed the Lord's Church to be organized and the Restoration to move forward. It has empowered His true disciples to stand out prominently among their Christian neighbors, and it has endowed them with an element of singularity that distinguishes them from other denominations, allowing the line in the sand separating His covenant faithful from the world to be more clearly defined.

> Christmas is
> the season of the
> year when, as a welcome
> change, it is not politically
> incorrect, nor is it socially
> unacceptable, to love
> as Jesus did.

We adopt the substantive lifestyle of Zion in contrast to the transparency of Babylon. We learn to trust in Zion's grip on reality even as Babylon grasps for straws in the confusion of an illusion that is of its own making. We know that Zion deals in spiritual absolutes even as Babylon tosses to and fro in a vacuum of moral relativism. We witness the focus of Zion as well as Babylon's congenital spiritual short-sightedness. We are comforted that Zion is grounded on the bedrock of principles, even as Babylon basks in a false sense of security, mistaking its values for principles, and thinking that all is well.

> Christmas is the season of the year when we take stock of the previous twelve months, to avoid getting caught up in, and absorbed by, our own accomplishments.

How quickly are we "lifted up in pride; yea, how quick to boast." (Helaman 12:5). And yet, how great an example were the Wise Men of the East. They may have been the Magi of Zoroastrianism, wearing the trappings of wealth, enjoying position, and bearing costly gifts, but it was their humility that we remember. It was their submissive nature that compelled them to make the arduous journey from the East, all the way to Bethlehem. It is significant that, over 2,000 years after their pilgrimage, we still refer to them as "Wise Men."

Christmas is the season of the year when we shed our pretentions, discard our skepticism, and cast off our affectations, allowing ourselves to be carried away on the pulsing waves of the Spirit into streams of revelation and carried along in the quickening currents of direct experience with God.

When we feel something, we can express it. If we can't, we don't feel it strongly enough. "Once, in a sermon, B.H. Roberts described Christ and the raising of Lazarus. So vivid were his images, and so moving his presence, that the audience was carried with him. When, in a loud voice, he repeated the Master's words: 'Lazarus, come forth!' the entire congregation involuntarily came to its feet." (Truman Madsen, "Defender of The Faith," p. 355).

Christmas is the season of the year that invites us to recalibrate our energies and refocus our priorities.

It is a time of re-evaluation, recommitment, renewal, rebirth, and revelation. Christmas helps us to concentrate on principles of perfection that are taught by legal administrators who receive their authority from heaven.

Christmas
is the season
of the year when
all are welcome
at our hearth
and home.

When the Babe of Bethlehem had grown into a man, He reproved the Pharisees, who had criticized His association with "the wrong crowd" consisting of publicans and sinners. He taught: "They that be whole need not a physician, but they that are sick." He rebuked them for their criticism of his old-fashioned house-calls and compassionate hospice care, saying: "I am not come to call the righteous, but sinners to repentance." (Matthew 9:11-13).

Christmas is the season of the year when we take to heart the lesson from the children's poem that begs: "Teach me all that I must do." ("I Am a Child of God").

About fifteen million people in the world die of starvation each year. That's one person every 2.1 seconds. Currently, while around 146,000 people die every day (about 100 a minute) only about 250,000 eternal lives are saved each year (about 1 every two minutes) because they have been taught the principles of the Gospel. This is a number that has remained relatively steady for many years. If we did it the Lord's way, on the other hand, the world could be saved in eleven years: say, 5 million this year, 10 million next year, 20 million the next year, 40 million the following year, and so on, until in the eleventh year, over five billion of Heavenly Father's children could be taught the Plan of Salvation, if each member would just share the Gospel with one other person every year. That would be a great Christmas present!

Christmas is
the season of the year
when conditions are ripe
for the children of God
to be weaned from
milk to meat.

There are three elements of effective teaching that relate to core curriculum. They are 1) teach key doctrine, 2) extend an invitation to action, and 3) describe promised blessings. Thomas S. Monson offered what could be thought of as a Christmas message when he said: "The goal of gospel teaching . . . is not to 'pour information' into the minds of class members. Its aim is to inspire the individual to think about, feel about, and then do something about living gospel principles" (C.R., 10/1970).

> Christmas is the season of
> the year when our service and
> sacrifices are put in perspective
> and we realize how puny our
> efforts really are, unless
> we invite the Spirit to
> show us the way.

Without the Spirit to guide us, we must remain as the "very cautious man who never laughed or played, who never risked, who never tried, who never sang or prayed. And when, one day, he passed away, his insurance was denied, for since he never really lived, they claimed he never died." (Mark Barsouna). However, when we do have the Spirit to be with us, when Christmas puts our teaching efforts in perspective, we pour ourselves into the task so that we can be lifesavers. We focus on the doctrine of Christ and love those whom we teach, as does our Heavenly Father. We have such a passion for our message that those whom we teach find it hard to resist our invitation to action. We bear personal testimony that is based on our own experiences relating to the anticipated blessings, and make them seem worth working and fighting for. We can be saviors on Mount Zion through our teaching of key doctrine. (See Obadiah 1:21).

> Christmas is
> the season of the
> year when it dawns on
> us that the oracles of
> God are all marked
> men and women.

Satan has hired assassins whose sole mission is to destroy faith, particularly of those who are in a covenant relationship with the Lord. The powerful antidote to the telestial trauma caused by the venom of Satan's snake bites is found within the story of Christmas. Those who have been commissioned to lift others up follow the pattern established by the Savior; they stand on higher ground and lose their lives in service. In return, the supernal gift of Christmas blesses them with the assurance that they will find them again.

> Christmas is the season of the year when our desire to walk the covenant path is intensified.

The danger in doing nothing is that we don't know when we are finished. Our good intentions may be noble, but achievement is the hallmark of progress. Our capacity to change is powered by more than the AA batteries we find among the gift wrap on Christmas morning. It is prompted by our intrinsic sense of nobility, for we are the sons and daughters of a King.

Christmas
is the season
of the year when
"an angel of the Lord
came upon them, and the
glory of the Lord shone
round about them."
(Luke 2:9).

The quiet whisperings of the Spirit reassure us that "surely, whoever speaks to me in the right voice, him or her I shall follow, as the waters follow the moon, silently with fluid steps, anywhere around the globe." (Walt Whitman, "Leaves of Grass").

Christmas is the
season of the year
when we recognize the
truth in the statement made
by the Savior: "Inasmuch as ye
have done it unto the least
of these, my brethren, ye
have done it unto me."
(Matthew 25:40).

With patience, we bear our stripes for the Savior, and it is for Him that we go the second mile. Fueled by the power of His example, we love our brethren, His brethren, as ourselves. Because He awakens us to re-commitment, we are alive to our responsibilities, as we minister to the weak, the sick and infirm, wash the wounds of the injured, and proudly bear His name.

Christmas is the season of the year when we give gifts of gold, frankincense, and myrrh, and recognize that these are mere shadows of the greatest Gift of all: the Christ Child.

The gift of His grace is granted unto us proportionately as we conform to the standard of personal righteousness that is part of His Gospel Plan. Thus, we are commanded to "grow in grace" (D&C 50:40), until we are sanctified and justified "thru the grace of our Lord and Savior Jesus Christ." (D&C 20:30-32). It is in this sense that Nephi declared that we are saved by grace only "after all we can do," which is primarily to repent of our sins. (2 Nephi 25:23).

> Christmas is the
> season of the year
> when the cynicism of
> Babylon is overcome
> by the charity
> of Zion.

Over two thousand times, Christmas morning has renewed the promise of a God-centered earth "full of the knowledge of the Lord, as the waters cover the sea." (Isaiah 11:9). "No form of government and no level of material well-being will save us. We will be redeemed only when towers fall and Bethlehem triumphs over Babylon. What is at stake, finally, is not only intelligence, but also feeling. We have to change our hearts." (Abba Eban).

> Christmas
> is the season of the
> year when the Spirit gives
> us the courage to testify to
> all the world, as well as to
> our next-door neighbors,
> of the divine mission
> of the Savior.

We enjoy a special, covenant relationship with God; we are "a chosen generation, a royal priesthood, an holy nation, (and) a peculiar people." (1 Peter 2:9). We privately bear the sacred emblems of that covenant, and especially at Christmas time, we publicly testify that God lives.

> Christmas is the season of the year when His disciples passionately embrace the Gospel with its ordinances and covenants, that they might equally embrace His divine nature.

When we first reach out to touch the face of God, the real journey to Christ has only just begun. We must press forward with complete dedication and steadfastness, with confidence and a firm determination, having a perfect brightness of hope and a love of God and of all men. We feast upon the word of Christ, receiving strength and nourishment from the scriptures, and endure to the end in righteousness. We receive the grace of God and the hope of eternal life, which is the greatest of all the gifts of Christmas. (See 2 Nephi 31:20).

Christmas is the season of the year when the words of the Savior echo in our ears: "I was in the beginning with the Father, and am the Firstborn." (We take that part for granted. But the second part expands our comprehension to infinite proportion). "Ye were also in the beginning with the Father." (D&C 93:21 & 23).

The purpose of our lives is to so live that we qualify to regain the glory of our former home. We remain "at work with our hands to the plough and our faces to the future," reflected Sir William Mulock. "The shadows of evening lengthen about us, but morning is in our hearts. The testimony I bear is this: The castle of enchantment is not yet behind me, but is before me still, and daily I catch glimpses of its battlements and towers. The best of life is always further on. The real lure is hidden from our eyes, somewhere beyond the hills of time." (A Complimentary Luncheon to The Right Honourable Sir William Mulock, at the Empire Club of Canada, 2/13/1930).

> Christmas
> is the season of
> the year when we see the
> fulfillment of prophecy, that
> the government of God
> should be established
> among men and
> women.

In some ways, it is easier to govern society than ourselves. Of one ancient political leader it was candidly recorded: "And he did do justice unto the people, but not unto himself because of his many whoredoms; wherefore he was cut off from the presence of the Lord." (Ether 10:11.) "We can cater to mortal constituencies but lose the support of the one Elector who matters!" (Neal A. Maxwell, "Ensign," 7/1982). The Christmas holidays are like spiritual smelling-salts that arouse our conscious awareness of life's meaning and purpose.

Christmas is
the season of the
year when the U.S. Postal
Service receives thousands
of letters addressed
to "Santa Claus."

These are from children asking him for specific presents. (No-one keeps track of the number of "thank-you letters" Santa receives after the holidays from the grateful recipients of all those gifts.) But when we remember, instead, to express gratitude to Heavenly Father for the blessings He showers upon us, glowing sparks are kindled that grow into a celestial fire that sustains us in moments of doubt and darkness.

Christmas is the season of the year when we see in the little family of Joseph, Mary, and Jesus, the prototype of our own nuclear relationships.

"Why should it surprise us that life's most demanding tests as well as its most significant opportunities for growth usually occur within marriage and the family? How can revolving-door relationships, by contrast, be a real test of our capacity to love?" (Neal A. Maxwell, "Ensign," 7/1982).

Christmas
is the season
of the year that teaches
us that there are no "God
forsaken" souls, for all have
access to the Light of Christ,
and to the intimate comfort
of prayer. The only reason
we may not feel close to
Him is because it is we
who have moved,
and not He.

The story is told of two friends at Auschwitz Concentration Camp during World War II. One felt completely alone and forgotten, his situation hopeless. The other knelt down each morning to pray, and his companion finally berated him for it. "For what could you possibly thank God, given our terrible circumstances?" he asked. His friend simply replied, "I thank God every day that He didn't make me like them."

Christmas is the season of the year when we can all lower our defensive shields and believe in a story that might seem incredulous to us at other times.

All of us have "limiting beliefs," those stories we tell ourselves that cause us to sabotage our own best intentions and efforts. They haunt us as they diminish our abilities and obscure our goals. Most people don't realize it's possible to change them, and for that matter, may not even realize that they have them. Breaking free from limiting beliefs can unleash the power of our potential. In fact, Christmas is full of magic patiently waiting for our wits to grow sharper so that we can fall under the spell of the Newborn King.

Christmas is the season of the year when we pause to reflect on our relationship with "a virgin espoused to a man whose name was Joseph, of the house of David." (Luke 1:27).

She was a young woman who had obviously accepted her special calling with profound sobriety, and who was prepared to sacrifice other opportunities for self-fulfillment to instead nurture her Newborn Son. As a writer once asked: "Are women who enjoy motherhood intellectual dropouts? What would have become of the human race had Eve rejected motherhood in favor of pursuing a more gratifying career in the already promising apple industry?" ("Time Magazine," 9/30/1974).

Christmas is the
season of the year when
we acknowledge the Lord as
our Elder Brother, Who was in
the beginning with our Father,
and is the Firstborn of all
of His spirit children.
(See D&C 93:21).

He came into the world to generate enthusiasm in His disciples, create confidence in their hearts, and show them how He could fix their mistakes rather than assigning blame. He was certain of His authority, but still delegated responsibility. He knew how, but more often showed how. He never reduced work to drudgery, but rather elevated it to excitement. Instead of concentrating power, he generated co-operation. He never drove His disciples forward, but was always out in front of them leading them to green pastures and still waters.

Christmas is the season of the year that unleashes the divine potential of His disciples, who are "distinguished for their zeal towards God, and also towards men." (Alma 27:27).

Disciples are not only honest and upright, but they are also firm in the faith. Christmas "demands strong minds, great hearts, true faith and ready hands," wrote Josiah Holland, "those whom the lust of office does not kill; those whom the spoils of office cannot buy; those who possess opinions and a will; those who have honor; those who will not lie; those who can stand before a demagogue and damn his treacherous flatteries without winking; those who live above the fog in public duty and in private thinking."

Christmas is the season of the year when the scriptures that testify of the birth of the "Only Begotten Son, Who was in the bosom of the Father, even from the beginning," beckon us to find wisdom and hidden treasures of knowledge.
(D&C 76:13).

The process demands a search for those pearls that may not be readily discernable after only a cursory glance. We must all beware how we handle the oracles of God, "lest they are accounted as a light thing, and (we) are brought under condemnation thereby, and stumble and fall when the storms (of a winter devoid of the Christmas spirit) descend." (D&C 90:5).

Christmas is the season of the year when "the great division among the people" that was foretold by Nephi of old is most apparent. (2 Nephi 30:10).

In the Last Days, combatants are once again forming into diametrically opposed camps with increasingly polarized ideologies. Ultimately, the story of the birth of Christ penetrates to our innermost parts, dividing truth from error, separating the sheep from the goats, and the wheat from the tares.

Christmas
is the season
of the year when the
doctrine of Christ speaks to
our spirits, urging us to press
forward with steadfastness and
a perfect brightness of hope, and
a love of God and of all men,
feasting upon the scriptures
and enduring to the end.
(See 2 Nephi 31:20).

Every Gospel principle carries within itself its own witness of truth. "The Lord giveth light unto the understanding, for he speaketh unto men according to their language." (2 Nephi 31:3). Fluency in the universal language of the Spirit enables every nation, kindred, tongue, and people to equally comprehend the story of the first Christmas. (See Revelation 14:6).

Christmas is the season of the year when He Who was born to be the Light of the World and the Light of Life stands out as "a bright and morning star" that even today shines above all others in the heavens. (Revelation 22:16).

When our lives are patterned after His, we are on a solid footing. He told the Saints in Zarahemla: "Ye know the things that ye must do in my church; for the works which ye have seen me do that shall ye also do." (3 Nephi 27:21). "Where is Heaven?" asked the poet. "Is it very far? I would like to know if it's beyond the brightest star." (Janice Kapp Perry). The answer to her questions is that heaven is right before us.

> Christmas is the season of the year that cohesively and coherently draws together all of the scriptures that would otherwise independently testify of the divinity of Jesus of Nazareth; it is a time when the doctrine of Christ may be expounded in one. (See 3 Nephi 23:14).

Whether our Gospel instruction comes in biblical teachings or Book of Mormon instruction, commandments in the Doctrine & Covenants, exhortation from the pages of The Pearl of Great Price, or from pulpits aflame with faith, it is the same. God's word is established in the mouths of two or three credible witnesses. Christmas brings these diverse voices together, in one.

Christmas is the season of the year when everyone, by divine design, may touch the hem of the Savior's garment, and feel the influence of the Holy Spirit of God.

Lorenzo Snow said of his baptism of the Spirit: "It was a tangible immersion in the heavenly element, the Holy Ghost; and even more real and physical in its effects upon every part of my system than the immersion by water, dispelling forever, so long as reason and memory last, all possibility of doubt or fear in relation to the fact that the Babe of Bethlehem is truly the Son of God; also the fact that He is now being revealed to the children of men, and communicating knowledge, the same as in Apostolic times." ("Biography and Family Record of Lorenzo Snow").

> Christmas is the season of the year when we sit at the feet of the prophets and feel their vibrant testimonies of the Savior.

It is one thing to rehearse the dealings of God with His children in ancient times. To be sure, those events that were prophesied long ago and have long since come to pass serve to confirm our faith and strengthen our testimonies. But it is quite another thing to witness the prophetic power of latter-day servants of God who speak in the name of the Lord and reveal truth that has been hidden from the world. Joseph Smith promised the Saints both personal and institutional revelation, when he said: "God shall give unto you knowledge by his Holy Spirit; yea, by the unspeakable gift of the Holy Ghost, that has not been revealed since the world was, until now." (D&C 121:26).

> Christmas is
> the season of the
> year when we catch a
> glimpse of what it
> means to enjoy
> God's Rest.

His Rest is born of a settled conviction of the truth in our minds. Today, we may enjoy the peace of Christmas by coming to an understanding of the truths of the Gospel and by then conforming our lives to celestial principles. The peace that surpasses all understanding eludes the world, although it is right under its nose. The Spirit, that is alien to its selfish nature, promises to bestow upon the Saints the gift of a flowing river of revelation, upon whose currents they will undertake the journey of a lifetime.

Christmas is the season of the year when the Hope of Israel renews the promise of our spiritual re-birth.

As we look around, it seems the world has gone mad, but the Church remains an island in the storm, and Christmas beckons us to come in from the cold to find refuge from the icy wind of life's uncertainties. It speaks a language of stability, direction, and purpose to those who are unsure, disoriented, and hesitant. Of those who embrace the spirit of Christmas, it might be said: "The stars fade away, the sun himself grows dim with age, and nature sinks in years; But thou shalt flourish in immortal youth, unhurt amidst the war of elements, the wreck of matter, and the crash of worlds." (Joseph Addison, "Cato," Act 5, Scene 1).

Christmas is
the season of the
year that reminds us
that we needed to leave
the nursery of our spiritual
educational experience, in
order to embark upon
our real journey
Home.

"Think of stepping on shore and finding it heaven. Of taking hold of a hand and finding it God's hand. Of breathing a new air and finding it celestial air. Of feeling invigorated and finding it immortality. Of passing from storm and tempest to the unbroken calm of God's Rest. Of waking up and finding it Home." (Robert Selle).

> Christmas is the season of the year when we may count ourselves fortunate, not that we may soon be the recipients of telestial bells and whistles, but that, instead, we may be "exceedingly rich, because of (our) prosperity in Christ." (4 Nephi 1:23).

We remember the Wise Men, who had the credentials to enter the royal palace of proud King Herod and boldly ask: "Where is he that is born King of the Jews? For we have seen his star in the east, and are come to worship him." (Matthew 2:1-2). Their gift was a lesson that the wealthy, the learned, the notable, and the foreign born may come unto Christ and that temporal trinkets pale in comparison to the gifts of testimony and burning faith. Wise men and women everywhere are as white-hot sparks struck off the divine anvil of God.

Christmas is the
season of the year when we
realize that our journey to the
manger outside of Bethlehem
may first lead us through
our own Gethsemane.
(See D&C 122:8).

"Every man must follow the same course whether he be rich or poor, educated or untrained, prince or pauper, or king or commoner. There is only one way. It is a long road spiked with thorns and briars and pitfalls and problems." (Spencer W. Kimball).

Christmas is the season of the year when the Spirit confirms that the Savior was the God Jehovah before His birth in Bethlehem (Hebrew: Bet Lehem or House of Bread), and that, in a sense, He too was Born Again, but as the Gift of God, the Son of David.

Jesus taught Nicodemus the Christmas morning message that except we are born again, we cannot see the kingdom of God." (See John 3:3). Peter later taught the principle of "being born again, not of corruptible seed, but of incorruptible, by the word of God." (1 Peter 1:23). His fellow apostle John confirmed: "Whatsoever is born of God overcometh the world." (1 John 5:4). These are they who are insulated from the carnality, sensuality, and devilishness of men, insomuch that "whosoever is born of God sinneth not." (1 John 5:18). These are they to whom Jesus Christ gave "power to become the sons of God, even to them that believe on his name: Which were born, not of blood, nor of the will of the flesh, nor of the will of man, but of God." (John 1:12-13).

> Christmas is the season of the year when we feel an upward thrust within ourselves. Our innate urge to go the second mile is "a gift of spiritual independence that removes the veil of insensitivity to our destiny."
> (Richard Gunn).

It was the Dominican priest Henri Didón who, in the opening ceremony of a school sporting event in 1881, first expressed the words that would later become the motto of Olympians: "Citius, Altius, Fortius!" (Faster, Higher, Stronger!) At Christmas, our souls are illuminated by the burning Spirit of God, and we can no longer remain passive. As Parley P. Pratt declared: "I have received the holy anointing, and I can never rest until the last enemy is conquered, death destroyed, and truth reigns triumphant." ("Deseret News" 4/30/1853).

Christmas is
the season of the year
when, rather than shuttering our
windows and bolting our doors, we throw
them open to our friends and neighbors
and invite them in, that together we
might enjoy not only the sunlight
streaming in across our faces,
but also the warmth of
our fellowship.

"Present levels of performance are not acceptable, either to ourselves or to the Lord. In saying that, I am not calling for flashy, temporary differences in our performance levels, but for a quiet resolve to lengthen our stride." (Spencer W. Kimball, "Ensign," 11/1974).

Christmas is
the season of
the year when our
hearts are softened
by lovely renditions of
hymns of praise and
thanksgiving.

"Glories stream from heaven afar; heavenly hosts singing alleluia!" ("Silent Night"). Such sweet symphonies penetrate to our core, touch our spirits, resonate with our heart-strings, illuminate our minds, and motivate us to action.

Christmas
is the season of the year
when spiritual realities enjoy
center stage and are illuminated
from above. That light is of God,
and it will grow brighter and
brighter until the children
of God are perfected
in Christ.

Too often, we are "clever, interesting, and brilliant, but we lack one of the three dimensions of life. We have no upward reach. Our conversation sparkles, but it is frivolous and often flippant. Our talk is witty, but is often at the expense of high and sacred things." (Charles Jefferson).

Christmas
is the season of
the year that charges
our faith to receive the
gift of hope; wherein we
make a more determined
effort toward "progress to
an endless advancement
in eternal perfections."
(Brigham Young).

As we seek to improve ourselves, we remember that if we always do what we always did, we'll always get what we always got. Even if we're on the right road, we're going to get run over if we just sit there. Those who seek improvement have high ideals that "are like stars. We will not succeed in touching them with our hands. But, like the seafaring man in the desert of waters, we choose them as our guides, and following them, we will reach our destiny." (Carl Shurz, "B.Y.U. Studies," 16:4).

Christmas is the
season of the year when
we can see in the birth of the
Savior perceptible hints of our
own divinity, for trailing
clouds of glory have we
all come, "from God,
Who is our Home."
(Wordsworth).

Cosmic background radiation is a footnote of creation, and while physicists may see in it nothing more than evidence of the Big Bang, we know that our blood runs hot because we are part of God's universe. "The very molecules that make up our bodies are traceable to the crucibles that were once the centers of high-mass stars that exploded into the galaxy, seeding pristine gas clouds with the chemistry of life. We are all connected to each other biologically, to the earth chemically, to the rest of the universe atomically", and to God eternally. (Neil deGrasse Tyson).

> Christmas is the
> season of the year
> when we overcome our
> prejudices and reach
> out to those whom
> we might, in other
> circumstances,
> avoid.

With an unflagging positive mental attitude, the young nephew of Ebenezer Scrooge said: "I never knew my mother. But I hope to know Scrooge one day." (Charles Dickens, "A Christmas Carol"). It might have been said of Scrooge before his epiphany, that "he had scribed a circle that drew others out; that he considered his neighbors heretics, rebels, and things to flout! But love and his nephew had the wit to win. They scribed a circle that drew him in." (See Edwin Markham, "Outwitted"). The rest of the story, as they say, is history.

Christmas is the
season of the year
when we give thanks for
our bishops, fathers, mothers,
teachers, ministers, friends, and
neighbors, who have selflessly and
even unconsciously strengthened
our testimonies and nurtured
our struggling spirits so that
we might have a more sure
witness of the Savior.

Sir Isaac Newton invented calculus, defined the laws of motion, and has been credited with an astonishing list of other accomplishments. Asked how he was able to do it all, he simply replied: "I stood on the shoulders of giants."

Christmas
is the season
of the year when
our thanksgiving,
that gains momentum
through late November,
is further intensified
until it reaches a
feverish pitch by
December
25th.

What if we have only mastered the cultivation of gratitude late on the Christmas afternoons of our lives, when it is almost too late? "Don't be discouraged if you haven't been an especially grateful person," counseled Joseph Wirthlin. "Rejoice, and think of what an impression you will make on those who thought they knew you! Think of how delightfully surprised they will be" when they realize how you have changed! ("B.Y.U. Devotional," 10/31/2000).

> Christmas is
> the season of the year
> when we yield to the Savior
> that with which it is most
> difficult for us to part:
> our former selves.

In the novel "The Picture of Dorian Grey," by Oscar Wilde, a particularly handsome young man's portrait degenerates over time in response to his moral depravity and self-indulgence, while at the same time his face retains its alabaster innocence. After many years of decadence have taken a mighty toll on his character, he loses his mind, grabs a knife and attacks the picture that with such stark realism and accuracy has reflected his mounting debauchery. The servants of the house awaken to a cry from the locked room and break down the door. There lies the body of an unrecognizable old man, stabbed in the heart, his face withered and decrepit. By the ring on his finger, they identify the disfigured corpse as their master. Beside the emaciated figure is the picture of Dorian Gray that has reverted to its original loveliness.

Christmas is
the season of the
year when we turn
to Advent as a period
of spiritual preparation.
In our mind's eye, each one
of the doors of the calendar,
beginning with fasting, prayer,
and repentance, and concluding
with anticipation, hope, and joy,
blesses us with a confirmation
that the story that has been
so beautifully recounted
in Luke Chapter 2
is true.

Of that which is revealed each time a door of our Advent Calendar is opened, Joseph Smith wrote: "This is good doctrine. It tastes good. I can taste the principles of eternal life, and so can you. They are given to me by the revelations of Jesus Christ; and I know that when I tell you these words of eternal life as they are given to me you taste them, and I know that you believe them." ("Teachings," p. 355).

Christmas is the season of the year that invites us to calibrate our moral compass according to the light that has gathered in the East. Its needle does not point to Santa's workshop at the North Pole, but instead to the way we should go, for it works according to our faith. (See Alma 37:40).

A good mariner can read the weather like a book and can focus his nautical skills to trim his sails and set a course that will lead him unerringly to safe harbor. The same wind that might cause a less seaworthy craft to founder will fill the sails of the vessel of a skilled seafarer. Such a helmsman does not necessarily see the port that is his destination, for sometimes it is beyond the horizon, and at other times the tack of the vessel appears to be taking his ship away from its objective. But if good seamanship prevails, and correct principles are followed, even in the face of steady headwinds, storms, shoals, and hidden reefs, the landfall is always sure.

Christmas is the
season of the year
when even our most
faltering prayers
bind us to the
Infinite.

"The builder who first bridged Niagara's gorge, before he swung his cable shore to shore, sent out across the gulf his venturing kite, bearing a slender cord for unseen hands to grasp upon the further cliff and draw a greater cord, and then a greater yet, 'til at last across the chasm swung The Cable – then the mighty bridge in air. So may we send our little timid thoughts across the void, out to God's reaching hands. Send our love and faith to thread the deep, thought after thought, until the little cord, and we, are anchored to the Infinite." (Edwin Markham).

Christmas
is the season
of the year when
we open our scriptures
to Luke, to reverently and
rapturously repeat the words
of sounding joy down to the
last detail, until it becomes
The Greatest Story Ever
Told.

The words of the Christmas story "are not of men, but of me," said the Savior, "for it is my voice which speaketh them unto you; for they are given by my Spirit unto you, and by my power you can read them one to another; Wherefore, you can testify that you have heard my voice, and know my words." (D&C 18:34-35).

Christmas is the season of the year that fosters the gift of spiritual interdependency. In our early stage of maturation, we lean upon others as we nurture our own testimonies of Jesus Christ. Later, the Holy Ghost helps us to quickly move thru the next stage, that of independency, without suffering significant damage, so that we may finally be perfected in Christ as our Heavenly Father completes His work and Glory. (See Moses 1:39).

The Savior urged those in bondage to go the second mile, doubling their stride, to remove the veil of insensitivity to their destiny. When we are all wrapped up in ourselves, we make very small packages. Selfishness destroys our moral fiber and our capacity to feel, while the selfless nature of Christmas builds our character and our capacity to love. His work becomes ours; to bring to pass our immortality and eternal life. (See Moses 1:39).

Christmas
is the season
of the year when
we pray for the strength
to be firm and unflinching
as we stare directly into the face
of evil. We recall that the Mount of
Temptation is less than 18 miles from
Bethlehem, which is a distance that
can be dangerously covered in
the blink of an eye if we are
moving at the breakneck
pace of telestial
traffic.

We pray that we might be uncompromisingly full of faith when we face both adversity and the Adversary; that we might remain as humble and tender as children; that we might be self-effacing and embarrassed if we were to be held up as role models; that we might be sensitive to the whisperings of the Spirit, and that we might influence others to deepen their own testimonies of the divinity of the Savior, at Christmas time.

Christmas is
the season of the year
when we realize that, "to
be great in the kingdom of
God is to do service and
take pain for others."
(William Tyndall).

When we do so, we give of our wealth unto our kindred, unto orphans, and the poor, and the wayfarer, and to the beggar, and for the release of captives; and we observe prayer, and when we have covenanted, we fulfill our covenant; and we are patient in adversity and hardship, and in times of violence. (See: Koran, ii;177).

Christmas is the season of the year when we "see what love the Father hath showed upon us, that we should be called His sons and His daughters." (William Tyndall).

Elohim is our Father, for we were born of Him as His spirit children. We acquired His spiritual qualities and characteristics and were raised by Him to maturity until we could progress no more. We then left His presence to fulfill our mission on earth, because there were some laws that pertained only to mortality that we could not obey, and so there were some blessings that were as yet unavailable to us. Having completed our passage to earth, we now make the journey to Christ, and when we reach our destination, we will have hope of a glorious resurrection and eternal life in the Celestial Kingdom of God.

*Christmas is
the season of the year
when, once again, the signs
accompanying the birth of
the Light of the World
include wonders
in heaven.*

We more easily appreciate eternity when we "slip the surly bonds of earth and dance the skies on laughter-silvered wings. We climb sunward and join the tumbling mirth of sun-split clouds. We wheel and soar and swing high in the silence. Hovering there, we chase the shouting wind along, and fling ourselves through footless halls of air. Up, up the long, delirious, burning blue we top the windswept heights with easy grace, where never lark, or even eagle flew. And, while with silent, lifting mind we tread the high untrespassed sanctity of space, we put out our hands, and touch the face of God." (John G. Magee, Jr., "High Flight").

Christmas is
the season of the
year when we hang our
stockings on the chimney with
care, and hope that they will be
overflowing with an assortment of
"goodies" on Christmas morning. For
the moment, we conveniently forget
that our Father in Heaven has
earned a "Master's" degree
in nutrition.

He knows exactly what sustenance is best for us, in what proportion, at what frequency, and in what quantity. The organically grown spiritual food that He provides is wholesome, delicious, and high in moral fiber content. At Christmas, when we receive in the mail yet another fruitcake gift from Aunt Bertha, let us remember that He would like to instead teach us how to recognize the more potentially dangerous empty calories of carnality, the solid fats and added sugars of sensuality, the nutritional deficiency of devilishness, and the malnourishing mold of misinformation.

Christmas is the season of the year when the sign was given, that "the heavenly Babe you there shall find to human view displayed, all meanly wrapped in swaddling bands, and in a manger laid." ("While Shepherds Watched Their Flocks").

The circumstances of His birth blessed Jesus of Nazareth with few temporal advantages. Nevertheless, during the first 30 years of His life, "he served under his father, and he spake not as other men, neither could he be taught; for he needed not that any man should teach him." (J.S.T. Matthew 2:25).

> Christmas is
> the season of the
> year when our own
> testimonies of the Savior
> and The Plan of our Father
> are silhouetted against the
> backdrop of the sweeping
> panorama of Luke
> chapter two.

For our part, we believe in Christ. We speak and testify of His foreordination to be the Redeemer of the world. In His baptism, He demonstrated by example the way for all to follow. He taught the truths of the Gospel in simplicity. In the Garden of Gethsemane, He demonstrated strength and compassion. The crucifixion was only an apostrophe; His death but a diacritical mark to allow His disciples to re-focus their attention on His resurrection and ascension into heaven. He is our Advocate with the Father, the Bread of Life, the Cornerstone of our creation, and the foundation of our existence. For these reasons and more, His birth in Bethlehem is the pivotal event around which time itself is measured and experiences are put in perspective.

Christmas
is the season
of the year when we
can visualize the Babe in
the manger and ponder the
awesome truth that "we (too)
are the children of God, and
if children, then ... heirs of
God, and joint-heirs" with
the Savior of the world.
(Romans 8:16- 17).

Within our hearts is the yearning to know: "Have we not all one father? Hath not one God created us?" (Malachi 2:10). "The Spirit itself beareth witness with our spirit, that we are (His) children." (Romans 8:16). We "are the sons (and daughters) of the living God" and will "receive a crown of glory that fadeth not away." (1 Peter 5:4 & Hosea 1:10). God uses the Christmas season to reaffirm the truth that "He is "the Father of all," not only of Jesus the Christ but also of all of the sons and daughters of men. (Ephesians 4:6).

Christmas is the season of the year when we sit down to dinner, and soberly think of another family gathering to which we have already been invited, that will take place in the not too distant future. We hope and pray that, in every sense, it will be a gathering of eagles.

Our place settings at the table have already been prepared. (See Psalms 23:5). Christmas critics who attempt to highlight the secular aspects of the season are sucking on a pickle rather than savoring a delicious feast of many courses. Christmas is a well-planned and meticulously prepared gala; its menu items are not designed to satisfy epicureans, but rather the unpretentious palates of those who eagerly anticipate culinary creations that have been blended into a perfectly homogenous, nutritious, and complimentary whole.

Christmas is the season of the year when we more comfortably hearken to the voice of the Spirit.

"The things which some men esteem to be of great worth, both to the body and soul, others set at naught and trample under their feet. Yea, even the very God of Israel do men trample under their feet. I say trample under their feet, but I would speak in other words; they set him at naught, and hearken not" to the story of that first Christmas. (1 Nephi 19:7).

> Christmas is
> the season of the
> year when the Hope
> of Israel steadies our
> trembling hands and
> our shaking knees.

We "have hope through the atonement of Christ and the power of his resurrection, to be raised up unto life eternal, and this because of (our) faith in him according to the promise." (Moroni 7:41). Hope is the inevitable reward of well-founded faith, when our lives are in harmony with Gospel principles. When we enjoy the fruits of faith to believe in the Christmas story, we consecrate our lives to the Savior, and throw ourselves upon the altar of His sacrifice, whose foundation is buttressed by a supernal display of divine direction. We rejoice in our unwavering confidence in the Spirit's capacity to drive us relentlessly forward. The faith to believe endows us with the settled conviction that His power to save has been unleashed in our behalf, to flow over our wounds as a healing balm, to prepare us to one day meet His penetrating gaze with clear and unashamed eyes.

Christmas is the season of the year when we recall how, during the Savior's ministry among the Nephites, they were baptized with fire and with the Holy Ghost.

It was truly a Pentecostal experience, for "they were encircled about as if it were by fire; and it came down from heaven, and the multitude did witness it, and did bear record; and angels did come down out of heaven and did minister unto them." (3 Nephi 19:14). It was as it had been during the Exodus, when the Lord commanded Moses: "Put off thy shoes from off thy feet, for the place whereon thou standest is holy ground. (For) I am the God of thy fathers, the God of Abraham, the God of Isaac, and the God of Jacob." (Exodus 3:5-6).

Christmas is the season of the year when, in northern climes, the earth is blanketed in white.

In language unique in the scriptures, Mormon recorded that those to whom the Savior ministered "were as white as the countenance and also the garments of Jesus; and behold the whiteness thereof did exceed all the whiteness, yea, even there could be nothing upon earth so white as the whiteness thereof." (3 Nephi 19:25). They had been symbolically purified in the redeeming blood of Christ and by His grace were saved.

> Christmas is the season of the year when we hear the bells peal, "and wild and sweet, the words repeat, of Peace on Earth, Good Will Toward Men." ("I Heard the Bells on Christmas Day").

There will be peace on earth only after the world begrudgingly looks to Zion as a living testament to the potential for goodness that is found in all of us. Babylon fails to recognize that the reward of faith is celestial surety, because it grovels in telestial tendencies. Babylon takes what it can get, while Zion stands for personal accountability. Even as Babylon shifts the blame in a flight from responsibility, it distantly admires the work ethic of Zion. At the end of the day, though, Zion's spiritual maturity sharply stands out against Babylon's juvenile irresponsibility.

> Christmas is the season of the year when we realize that it was Luke the pediatrician who documented for posterity the Savior's first baby-steps along the road that would eventually lead Him all the way to Gethsemane.

As toddlers, we all take halting steps in life's nursery, on our way to "becoming". We start out pretty much the same, although little boys are made of frogs and snails and puppy dog tails, and little girls are made of sugar and spice and everything nice. Particularly during the Christmas season, it's quite apparent that "little girls are made of daisies and butterflies and soft kitty cat purrs, and all the precious memories of times that once were. Little girls are made of angel's wings and giggles and a firefly's glow, and all the happy feelings, deep inside, that we all know. Little girls are made of cinnamon and bubbles and fancy white pearls, and snowflakes and rainbows and ballerina twirls. Little girls are made of sunshine and cupcakes and fresh morning dew." (Anonymous). And that's why little girls make our celebration of Christmas so special.

> Christmas is the season of the year when we realize that without the fatherhood of God, there can be no brotherhood of man. What is at stake is our very identity as His children. If we lose that, all must be forsaken. There would no longer be any reason for us to celebrate the birth of the Son of God.

Jesus loved all little children and taught us to emulate their qualities of innocence, trust, virtue, purity, and curiosity. They are amazing, and treat everyone with humility, gentleness, and kindness; they view the world enthusiastically, energetically and with wide-eyed wonder, awe, and anticipation. Is it any wonder that little children believe in Santa Claus? When we put away these childish things, we view life more dispassionately, but we sacrifice to some degree our joie de vivre and our ability to express ourselves naturally with unrestrained spontaneity. Because adults can be boring, the Savior emphasized: "Except ye be converted, and become as little children, ye shall not enter into the kingdom of heaven." (Matthew 18:1-2). (We can do that if we put Christ, and not Santa, back in Christmas).

Christmas is
the season of the year
when "you'd better not shout, and
you'd better not cry, you'd better not
pout, and I'm telling you why!" It
won't be long until Jesus Christ
comes to town, to establish
peace on earth for a
thousand years.

Christmas gently reminds us that we cannot avoid the question: "What think ye of Christ?" If we regard ourselves as His spiritual offspring, internalize His divine characteristics, and keep His memory alive at Christmas, how it will change our lives for the better! We will be prepared to meet Him in the skies when He comes again, to establish His millennial reign upon the earth, when the dawn of every waking day will be as yet another Christmas morning.

Christmas
is the season of
the year when our
heart-strings resonate
with the reality of heaven,
and the Spirit touches the
eyes of our understanding.
The veil between us and
forever becomes
very thin.

We feel the influence of the Lord's presence, no matter what direction we may be facing. As new creatures in Christ, He is always and forever before our faces. There is no path we may follow and no hiding place to which we may flee where we will not feel His profound influence. Every time we do a reality-check, we will find Him there. He is "Jesus Christ, the Great I Am, Alpha and Omega, the beginning and the end, the same which looked upon the wide expanse of eternity, and all the seraphic hosts of heaven, before the world was made. The same which knoweth all things, for all things are present before (His) eyes." (D&C 38:1-2). He knows when we are sleeping; He knows when we're awake. He knows when we've been good or bad, so we need to be good for goodness' sake. (Fred Coots & Haven Gillespie).

Christmas
is the season of
the year when, although
days grow shorter, twinkling
lights of every color and
description replace
the darkness
of night.

Christmas invites us to return to the secret garden of our childhood. Its celebration de-toxifies us from the cares and conditioning influences of the world and from the homogenization process that occurs throughout the rest of the year, when we are worn down by the vicissitudes of life. Christmas re-vitalizes us, as we are re-introduced to a Magical Kingdom that is the place where dreams really do come true. Wherever we may find ourselves at Christmas time, God helps it to become the happiest place on earth.

Christmas is the
season of the year
that awakens within
us the memory of our
own spiritual nursery,
even the Kingdom
of Heaven.

The world teaches us to be as "grown-up" as possible in order to succeed in life. Children are inundated with adult-themed messages: "Be a big boy!" and "Don't be a baby!" as if our maturation could be hastened. Those who have learned to roll with the punches are characterized as "seasoned veterans" and yet the process, far from tenderizing us, gives us a mental toughness and a thick skin that dulls our sensory and spiritual nerve endings. Christmas is a time when we can all let down our guard, reconnect with our divine center, return to the secret garden of our childhood, and simply enjoy the reason for the season.

> Christmas is the season of the year that invites us to more carefully consider our stewardship responsibilities; to ask ourselves if we are, in fact, our brothers' keeper.

Since Cain first made the inquiry, we have grappled with the question: "Am I my brother's keeper?" (Genesis 4:9). There is no better time than at Christmas to actively answer that question. As John Taylor encouraged us: "There are some Christian people in this world "who, if a man were poor or hungry, would say, let us pray for him. I would suggest a little different regimen for a person in this condition; rather take him a bag of flour and a little beef or pork. A few such comforts will do him more good than your prayers." (C.R., 10/1877). Such acts of quiet Christianity that are selflessly extended to the least of our brothers and sisters squarely address Cain's question. (See Matthew 25:40).

Christmas is the season of the year when "all the bells of Christendom roll along the unbroken song of Peace on Earth, Good Will Toward Men." ("I Heard The Bells on Christmas Day").

During the Christmas season, we are less judgmental, less suspicious, and more friendly. We are more accepting of others, often without reservation. We see others as neighbors and not as strangers. We are more trusting and speak without guile. We are more transparent and less prejudicial. We have fewer pretensions and are more genuine. We are less prone to rationalization and quicker to forgive. We are more honest, true, chaste, benevolent, and virtuous. Our faith is more vibrant, our hope more comprehensive, and our charity more pure.

Christmas is the
season of the year
when we visualize the
barnyard animals in the
musty shadows of the
stable outside
of town.

We see in all of God's creatures great and small, the instinctive drive to thrive in the midst of challenges. In spite of the serenity of the scene at the stable, Christmas also paints the portrait of God asking us to accept risk and move forward.

Christmas is the season of the year when we take a much-needed break from our everyday business. For a change, mankind becomes our affair. The common welfare is our business; charity, mercy, forbearance, and benevolence are our business. We see the dealings of our trade as nothing but a drop of water in the comprehensive ocean of our business. (See Charles Dickens', "A Christmas Carol").

The confiscation of their earthly treasures was the best thing that could have happened to Lehi's sons when they returned to Jerusalem. (See 1 Nephi 3 & 4). Divine tutorial training was woven into a seeming injustice when all the accumulated belongings of the family fortuitously fell into the hands of the unscrupulous Laban. They were uncomfortably taught to put the value of the world's goods in its proper perspective. God created this teaching moment to emphasize the importance of relying upon His power alone and not on the extrinsic worth of telestial trinkets to accomplish His purposes.

Christmas is the
season of the year when
we determine to give more than
just lip service to the invitation to
give "Glory to God on high!"
("Glory to God on High").

We cannot allow our prejudices to determine the depth of our compassion. We need to give glory to God on high, and then be about His business. Christmas is a time that invites us to venture out of our comfort zones into the uncharted territory of service.

Christmas is
the season of the
year when we bear our
afflictions more patiently,
knowing that the little Lord
Jesus had no crib for His bed, but
lay down His sweet head upon the
straw of the manger, sharing the
starry night with no-one except
Mary and Joseph, lowing cattle,
bleating sheep, cooing doves,
and clucking chickens.

In Dostoevsky's "The Brothers Karamazov," the Grand Inquisitor mused: "The ages will pass, and humanity will proclaim by the lips of their sages that there is no crime and there is no sin. There is only hunger." Christmas stands in bold opposition to that pessimistic outlook on life by addressing our primal need for sustenance with an opportunity to satisfy our spiritual hunger.

> Christmas is
> the season of the year
> that invites us to celebrate
> the inherent power in the weak
> things of the earth, and not to
> feel silly afterward, for
> having done so.

In the scriptures, we are admonished 439 times to prepare ourselves. Preparation means that we inventory our available resources and then make the best of it. The Lord Himself made preparation for 30 years before He commenced His ministry. In our Heavenly Father's divine design, our opportunities for preparation may involve life-long learning experiences. They have been tailor-made to suit our circumstances and our needs, whether we are professional athletes or practiced panhandlers, living in the fast or the slow lane, whether we have rags or riches, are leaders or lepers, late bloomers or early prodigies, venture capitalists or welfare recipients. Times and seasons change, but Christmas remains a time of preparation.

Christmas is the season of the year when we can light the world by sustaining our democratically elected representatives.

Even in the best of circumstances, government servants must not be left to their own devices without the guiding influence of the Spirit. Power tends to corrupt, and absolute power corrupts absolutely. When our hearts are set upon temporal things, spirituality suffers and moral compasses spin wildly out of control. Even those with whom we disagree deserve our prayers and God's blessings. Christmas is not a time for dissension, but for reconciliation.

Christmas is the season of the year when, in spite of our emphasis on giving; in spite of our recitation of the less-familiar question: "What did you give for Christmas?" we can still do nothing that would put the Savior of the world in our debt.

As King Benjamin taught, when we serve God with our whole heart and soul, we are free from dependence upon any other being. In regard to the poor, God transfers to them our indebtedness to Him. It is through them that He asks us to pay our debt to Him. Thus, a Zion Society is created from the raw material of righteous interdependency, obviating the need to ask the question: "What did you give for Christmas?" There will be no poor among us when we have learned how to celebrate Christmas well.

Christmas is
the season of the
year when we can see
how God has stacked the
deck in favor of His children,
making the reaffirmation of their
devotion to the newborn Babe
particularly easy. After all,
He is the reason for
the season.

Christmas invites us to keep ourselves clean and bright, for our clear eyes "are the windows through which we see the world." (George Bernard Shaw) "This above all, to thine own self be true," counseled Polonius to his son Laertes. "And it must follow, as the night the day, Thou canst not then be false to any man." (Shakespeare, "Hamlet," Act 1, Scene 3).

Christmas is
the season of the
year that blesses all true
believers with a special gift,
which is the ability to look within
themselves for a confirmation of their
faith. We come from our Heavenly Father
trailing clouds of glory, and when we
rediscover our footprints on that star
studded pathway that leads to our
divine center, we will be able to
retrace our steps to find our
way back Home.

Although, as Washington Irving brooded, it is the rule that "history fades into fable; fact becomes clouded with doubt and controversy; the inscription molders from the tablet; the statue falls from the pedestal," and "columns, arches and pyramids are but heaps of sand, and their epitaphs, nothing but characters written in the dust," yet the Christmas Story stands as a shining example of the divine model. ("Westminster Abbey").

Christmas is the season of the year when we trace the origin of the Hosanna Shout to the shepherds who were abiding their flocks by night, in the fields near Bethlehem. When suddenly, there was with the angels who had appeared to them "a multitude of the heavenly host praising God, and saying, Glory to God in the highest, and on earth peace, good will toward men." (Luke 2:13-14).

On March 27, 1836, the Kirtland Temple was dedicated, and at the close of the service the pattern for giving the Hosanna Shout was given. The Prophet Joseph wrote: "We sealed the proceedings of the day by shouting hosanna, hosanna, hosanna to God and the Lamb, three times, sealing it each time with amen, amen, and amen." (Documentary History of the Church 2:427-8.) This pattern of "hosanna," "to God and the Lamb," and "amen", repeated three times has formed the basis of the Hosanna Shout during all of Church history, down to the present time. What better time could there be to rehearse the Hosanna Shout in our minds, than on Christmas morning?

Christmas
is the season of the
year when we look up at the
stars in heaven, and realize that
Jesus Christ is the Architect of the
cosmos, including the "Pillars of
Creation," elephant trunks of
interstellar gas and dust
in the Eagle Nebula,
7,000 light years
from Earth.

In an 1857 sermon entitled "The Condescension of Christ," London pastor Charles Spurgeon used the phrase to describe both the physical world and the force stemming from the divine that binds it all together. "Now wonder, ye angels," Spurgeon wrote of the birth of Christ, "the Infinite has become an infant. He, upon whose shoulders the universe doth hang, nurses at his mother's breast; He who created all things and bears up the pillars of creation!"

Christmas is the season of the year when we look at the scarcity of the scene on the outskirts of Bethlehem, and realize that real poverty is having so many clothes, we haven't got a thing to wear. It is eating so well we have to think about going on a diet. It is being loaded down with toys at Christmas, and then being bored silly because there's nothing to do. It is never stopping to see the beauty of the world, especially at this season of the year.

As we celebrate Christmas, may we all have the wisdom to adopt for our personal use, our own modified version of the official motto of the Kingdom of Tonga, a poor island nation in the remote South Pacific: "Ko e 'Otua mo Tonga ko hoku tofi'a", "God and Tonga are my Inheritance".

Christmas is the season of the year when we resolve to try a little harder. We stand a little taller, walk a little straighter, are a little kinder, speak a little more gently, act a little more responsibly, think a little more carefully, serve a little more faithfully, listen a little more attentively, give a little more freely, receive a little more graciously, laugh a little more heartily, and cry a little more tenderly.

Blessed are those who realize that the biggest room in the world is the one for improvement. Ralph Waldo Emerson observed: "Success comes by design, and failure by default." Truly, if we fail to plan, we plan to fail, and the only place where success comes before work is in the dictionary. The best place to find helping hands is at the ends of our arms. When we use them to reach out to discover the true meaning of Christmas, they serve us well.

About The Author

Phil Hudson and his wife Jan have 7 children and over 25 grandchildren. They enjoy spending time with their family at their cabin nestled in the Selkirk Mountains, on the shore of Priest Lake, the crown jewel of North Idaho. Phil had a successful dental practice in Spokane, Washington for 43 years, before retiring in 2015. He has an eclectic mix of hobbies, and enjoys the out of doors. He always finds time, however, to record his thoughts on his laptop, and understands Isaac Asimov's response when he was asked: "If you knew that you had only 10 minutes left to live, what would you do?" He answered: "I'd type faster."

Phil received the inspiration to write this book while he and Jan were serving as missionaries for The Church of Jesus Christ of Latter-day Saints, in the Kingdom of Tonga. While there, they celebrated their 50th wedding anniversary.

By The Author

Essays

- Spray from the Ocean of Thought
- Ripples on a Pond
- Serendipitous Meanderings
- Presents of Mind
- Mental Floss
- Fitness Training for the Mind and Spirit

First Principles and Ordinances Series

- Our Hearts are Changed
- A Broken Heart and a Contrite Spirit
- One Hundred and One Reasons Why We Are Baptized
- That We Might Have His Spirit To Be With Us
- This Do in Remembrance of Me

Book of Mormon Commentary

- Volume One: Born In The Wilderness
- Volume Two: Voices From The Dust
- Volume Three: Journey To Cumorah

Doctrine & Covenants Commentary

    Volume One - Sections 1 - 34
    Volume Two - Sections 35 - 57

Minute Musings: Spontaneous Combustions of Thought

    Volume One
    Volume Two
    Volume Three

Calendars:

    In His Own Words: Discovering William Tyndale
    As I Think About The Savior
    Scriptural Symbols

Children's Books

    Book of Mormon Hiking Song
    Happy Birthday
    Muddy, Muddy
    The Hiawatha Trail: An Allegory
    The Little Princess
    The Parable of The Pencil
    The Strange Tale of Huckelberry Henry
    The Thirteen Articles of Faith

Doctrinal Themes

- Are Christians Mormon? Volume One
- Are Christians Mormon? Volume Two
- Christmas is The Season When…
- Dentistry in The Scriptures
- Gratitude
- Hebrew Poetry
- Hiding in Plain Sight
- One Hundred Questions Answered by The Book of Mormon
- The House of The Lord
- Without The Book of Mormon
- Writing on Metal Plates
- The Highways and Byways of Life Volume One
- The Highways and Byways of Life Volume Two
- The Highways and Byways of Life Volume Three

A Thought For Each Day of the Year

- Faith
- Repentance
- Baptism
- The Holy Ghost
- The Sacrament
- The House of the Lord
- The Plan of Salvation
- The Atonement
- Revelation
- The Sabbath
- Life's Greatest Questions

Professional Publications

- Diode Laser Soft Tissue Surgery Volume One
- Diode Laser Soft Tissue Surgery Volume Two
- Diode Laser Soft Tissue Surgery Volume Three

These, and other titles, are available from online retailers.

www.ingramcontent.com/pod-product-compliance
Lightning Source LLC
Chambersburg PA
CBHW060507240426
43661CB00007B/945